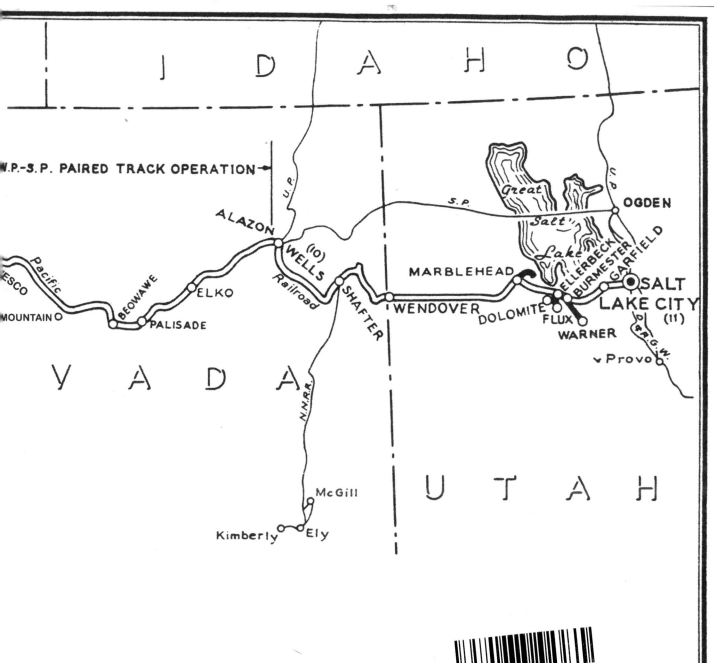

THE WESTERN PACIFIC RAILROAD COMPANY
SYSTEM

Scale in Miles

0 10 20 30 40 50 60 70 80 90 100

Western Pacific Locomotives and Cars

Volume 2

Steam · Diesel · Passenger · Freight

Patrick C. Dorin

TLC Publishing, Inc. 2006

Dedication

Dedicated to

Robert R. (Bob) Larson

Locomotive Engineer, Researcher, Photographer and Historian
For the Western Pacific Railroad and Long Time Friend

And to the Memory of

Dr. Dan Jacobson

Professor at Michigan State University
Who Taught Transportation Geography and
Inspired the Ideas and Framework for the Western Pacific Books

About the Author

Patrick Dorin has been interested in railroads since the age of two.

While attending undergraduate school at Northland College in Ashland, Wisconsin, he worked for the Great Northern Railway. Later he worked for the Elgin, Joliet and Eastern Railway, the Milwaukee Road, and the Duluth, Missabe & Iron Range Railway. His employment in the railroad industry included positions as a switchman, yard clerk, iron ore classification duties, operations and marketing research, customer service, and cost accounting. He has also served as a volunteer for the Duluth, Minnesota tourist railroads, the North Shore Scenic Railroad and the Lake Superior and Mississippi RR.

He holds degrees in business administration, marketing, elementary education and school administration including a Ph.D. from the University of Minnesota.

He recently retired as a school principal from the Superior, Wisconsin schools and has also taught marketing, operations research, transportation, management, Japanese Culture and School Administration for both the University of Wisconsin-Superior and the University of Minnesota-Duluth. He is currently doing operational design and product application research for a new Bi-model system for American Surface Lines.

Railroads continue to hold a strong fascination for Pat, and he has published over 40 books and nearly 40 articles on various aspects of railroad services and operations, companies, and equipment as well as other subjects.

Pat Dorin lives in Superior, Wisconsin with his wife Karen.

Table of Contents

International Standard Book Number: 1-883089-93-X

Design & Layout by

Megan Johnson

Johnson2Design, Rustburg, VA

Printed in USA

by Walsworth Publishing Co., Marceline, MO

Acknowledgements

The writer wishes to thank the following people for their kind assistance, encouragement and inspiration and for the use of a wide variety of materials and photographs for this new volume on the Western Pacific.

Bob Larson provided an incredible number of photographs as well as much other information for the two books by this writer for the WP. George Cockle also assisted with photographs and other detailed information. Tom Dixon of TLC Publishing encouraged this project as well as guiding the layout and final contents of the book. My wife Karen assisted with proof reading.

Many people provided a great deal of assistance with information and photographs including: Luther Miller from RAILWAY AGE, John Ryczkowski, Lou Schmitz, Tom Dorin, Harold K. Vollrath, Wayne Monger from the Altamont Commuter Express. Many photos came from the TLC Collection, Bob's Photos, the former Rail Photo Service, the former Western Pacific Photos and Burlington Route, and Jay Williams of Big Four Graphics.

Should an acknowledgment have been inadvertently omitted, the writer trusts that it will be found in the appropriate location within the text.

To all a huge thank you for without your kind assistance, the work on the Western Pacific would simply have not been possible.

Introduction

The research for the two Western Pacific books actually began over 30 years ago as a research project on the marketing mix and operations of the Western Pacific Railroad for a transportation class at Michigan State University. For a variety of reasons, the project did not evolve to a book project until the summer of 1988. The reasons could constitute a novel all by itself, but that is another story. Nevertheless, what was done as now turned into two books on the Western Pacific - thanks to our publisher and many others.

The specific purpose for this volume is to look at the overall train operations of the WP since its inception to its inclusion in the Union Pacific as the Feather River Division. Both freight and passenger services are covered as well as an additional pictorial review of the wide variety of motive power and rolling stock. The company is really a bonanza for the artistic work and operations for model railroads.

It is hoped that this book will provide the reader with something of the feel and the positive atmosphere of the WP, which was a very market orientated, meaning shipper and passenger needs, transportation company. Many businesses and organizations could learn much about the customer relations by studying the Western Pacific. In fact, it is interesting to note that the Wisconsin Central Railroad's marketing and operations philosophy and methods actually paralleled that of the Western Pacific. This says much about a sense of community, which is a critical component for successful organizations. It can be said that the WP's entire operating schema was based on customer needs.

Finally no subject can ever be totally covered. There is always something new and more to learn about anything. This book is no exception, but it hoped that it will fill a niche in the transport operations / railroad literature. Therefore, the writer has also included a short list of materials and sources for additional reading, research, education and just plain relaxation for the enjoyment of railroading.

As it is well known, the WP has been a part of the Union Pacific. Yet the WP lives on in the hearts of many people, and Western Pacific equipment continued (for awhile anyway) to carry the WP reporting marks with the UP insignia as the company entered into the 1990s. Such can still be observed as we move into the middle of the first decade of the 21st Century.

Patrick C. Dorin,
Superior, Wisconsin
September 1, 2003

Chapter 1

A HISTORICAL and GEOGRAPHICAL REVIEW

The Western Pacific Railroad was (and is) the western end of a transcontinental route between Chicago and San Francisco. Historically this route was made up of the WP from Oakland to Salt Lake City, Utah; the Rio Grande from Salt Lake City to Denver, and the Burlington Route from Denver to Chicago. The WP became part of the Feather River Division after the merger with the Union Pacific, and therefore became the western end of the UP and Chicago and North Western route between Chicago and Oakland. (And eventually the C&NW became part of the UP and it is now the Union Pacific route not only from Chicago to Oakland, but to Los Angeles, Portland and Seattle as well.)

The WP route was essentially a main line railroad with a few short branch lines in all three states served. The company operated a secondary main line from Keddie to Bieber, California. This segment was part of the famous "Inside Gateway," which competed with the coastal route of the Southern Pacific between California and the Pacific Northwest. The other parties of the "Inside Gateway" included the Santa Fe to the south and the Burlington Northern (former Great Northern trackage) to the north. Together the three railroads made up a coastal freight service between San Diego and Vancouver, British Columbia. The total mileage of the Western Pacific was approximately 1170 miles in the 1970s. The route remained relatively stable since the main line was completed in 1909 with the exception of the northern California extension which was built in 1931.

The birth of the WP lies in the fact that often when there was but one railroad through a geographical territory, it was often felt, both real and perceived, that the public was being exploited and at the mercy of the single carrier. Californians felt that such a situation existed with the Central Pacific, and

Western Pacific's "Ten-Wheeler" No. 94 has been preserved and operated for several special occasions over the past four decades plus since the late 1950s. Here it is under catenary at Rio Vista Junction, California (The Bay Area Electric Railway Association), in the company of an electric center cab switcher. The photo was taken on October 15, 1983. (Bob Larson Collection)

The next few photos show some of the Western Pacific environment and culture. The company operated many stations, both large and small, throughout the entire system. One of the largest was the Oakland depot on Third Street, which with its archways and other decor, could qualify for "Cathedralship." It was a great place to be and complete one's journey, especially on the "California Zephyr." This photo illustrates the depot as it was in 1959. (Bob Larson)

its eastward link with the Union Pacific in Utah. One such person was a young Scotchman by the name of Arthur W. Keddie. Keddie was a surveyor and an explorer. In the late 1860s, when the CP/UP was under construction, Keddie was exploring for a new mountain wagon route through the Sierra Nevada Mountains. While doing so, he discovered a potential rail route through the Feather River Canyon, which crossed the mountains at Beckworth Pass. This pass is more than 2000 feet lower than Donner Pass on the Southern Pacific. Keddie was able to determine that by use of Beckworth Pass, a railroad could be relatively free of steep grades. (1) However, all of the efforts to use this pass failed until about 1900 because of the oppositon by the Central Pacific. Although it had looked for a long time that no railroad would ever be built to compete with the CP, an unexpected turn of events was soon to change the picture.

Up to this time, Keddie was not able to secure any financial support for his proposed railroad. Meanwhile in 1901, George Gould added the Denver and Rio Grande Railroad to his system.

This meant that the Gould System extended from Buffalo, New York to Ogden and Salt Lake City. As the same time, the UP and the SP closed off the Utah Gateway to the Gould System. This meant that any freight traveling to the west coast (or west of Ogden) on the Gould System would have to be turned over to the UP at Omaha if it was to complete its journey. Gould was furious but he had no legal recourse except to find a way to build his own railroad

from the Rio Grande connection to the Pacific Coast. The case for the WP was building up. On the one hand, we have Keddie's dream of a Feather River Route for a line to compete with the giant Southern Pacific System. In addition most Californians felt that the SP monopoly had to be broken. On the other hand, we have Gould who needed a west coast route for his transcontinental freight business. All of the ingredients were in place for a new railroad company. What was needed was for Keddie and his associates to get together with Gould. By 1903 this teaming had been accomplished and on March 3, 1903, the Western Pacific Railway was organized in San Francisco with Walter J. Bartnett as President. (2)

Bartnett, however, was basically only a paper president for about two years. The Rio Grande Railroad underwrote $50 million in bonds for the WP's construction with the stipulation that a 1% compensated grade and curves of 10 degrees would be the maximum throughout the entire main line. (3) In 1905, the president of the Rio Grande, Edward T. Jeffrey, became president of the WP. Bartnett became Vice President and construction of the new railroad began the same year. The SP did not take the construction of the new railroad with any enthusiasm at all. On both the legal and physical fronts, the SP tried to stop the WP. The 1906 earthquake did not help either. But neither the physical force, the earthquake, or the courts of law stopped construction. The Western Pacific was

The WP's main line missed Reno, Nevada, but nevertheless rated an elegant building. Never graced by main line passenger service, the depot has seen activities involving such power as the Virginia and Truckee's 4-4-0, No. 12. (Bob Larson)

completed on November 1, 1909 as track foreman Leonarde diTomasse drove the last spike on Spanish Creek Bridge. (4) As track gangs from the east and the west met on this steel bridge, there were no ceremonies. In fact, the whole affair was done at such a low key it is surprising that there was even a photo taken of the event. Nevertheless, a new transcontinental railroad had been completed with a low level crossing of the Sierras at an elevation of 5000 feet. There were very few sharp curves and the line boasted a maximum grade of not over 1%.

The Western Pacific did indeed go to San Francisco, and this photo illustrates the 25th Street Yard with Alco switch engine number 507 standing guard at the old water tower. The yard was fairly extensive and once contained over 20 classification tracks. (Bob Larson)

Through freight service began 30 days later on December 1, 1909. (5) Passenger services began over the main line in August, 1910. Overall, the railroad had cost nearly $80 million to build and nearly ruined the Rio Grande's credit and prevented the construction of badly needed feeder lines and spur tracks. (6)

Moreover, nature did not favor the new railroad any more than it favored anyone or anything else. This added to the cost of operation. And one of the things that the WP had hoped for would be low operating costs through the low grade construction. However, such was not to be the case.

The WP constructed the main line across the southern end of the Great Salt Lake, which for eight miles is on a trestle or earth embankment in the water. In 1910, the Great Salt Lake was rising at the rate of about 2 feet per year. This in turn caused considerable damage to the trestle and earth embankment. In fact, the damage was so extensive that the WP actually considered running around the lake further south. This would have involved operating over the San Pedro, Los Angeles and Salt Lake Railroad. The railroad would also have had to build about 10 miles of new line to make a suitable connection with the main line west of the lake. (7) Eventually, the lake ceased to rise at the steady rate and the WP did not have to move the railroad further south.

During the first five years of WP history, freight traffic levels were very disappointing. This in turn brought financial difficulties for the Rio Grande, which owned 66% of the Western Pacific.

Despite the hard times, the WP did research with other companies. One project was with the National Safety Appliance Company. In 1915 that company installed a new automatic block signal system on a five mile section of single track line near Oroville. This worked wholly by audible and visual indications in the locomotive cab, and by automatic train stops. There were no visual roadside signals provided except for small light signals, one at each automatic stop location, called markers. Twenty locomotives were equipped with the signaling devices for use through the five mile section. (8) At the same time, there were many discussions concerning the safety of this new system, and many doubted it would work effectively. The WP did not install it over the entire main line as train frequency was not great enough to warrant its installation. Other railroads such as the Santa Fe, Southern Pacific and the Chicago and North Western eventually made extensive use of the system.

Meanwhile the financial condition continued to deteriorate. Finally in early 1916, the bond holders formed a new company, the Western Pacific Railroad Company. One June 18, 1916, the Western Pacific Railway was sold at foreclosure to the new Western Pacific Railroad Company. The new president was Charles M. Levey, who had been second vice president of the original company. (9)

The new management realized that positive action had to be taken to turn the tide. They actively went out and sought new business. Branch or feeder lines (which had been sorely needed) were either built or purchased. Rail traffic began to climb. Later in the year, the railroad purchased the Boca and Loyalton Railroad, which became the Loyalton Branch. A subsidiary line, the Deep Creek Railroad between Wendover and Gold Hill, Utah was built in March, 1917. This particular line was discontinued in July, 1939. The Indian Valley Railroad was completed in June, 1917. This line was owned jointly by the WP and the Engles Copper Mining Company, which was operated by the Western Pacific. It closed in 1938.

The Tidewater Southern Railway, an electric interurban line, was purchased in 1917. This line was under construction in 1911 and completed between Stockton and Modesto in 1912. It was extended to Turlock in 1916. Branch lines were built to Hilmar and Manteca in 1917 and 1918 respectively. Passenger service was discontinued in 1932 and the TS was dieselized in 1948. The Tidewater Southern served an important manufacturing, farming and wine producing region. (10) (See Chapter 2)

A book could be written on the WP's facilities alone. The company's facilities were built for transcontinental main line railroad work, and the Oroville Roundhouse was no exception. This view was taken from the cab of an "F" unit in 1963. (Bob Larson)

The WP's only narrow gauge venture, the southern section of the Nevada-California-Oregon Railway between Reno and the WP main line, was purchased in 1917. The line was relocated and standard gauged and became the Reno Branch on February 3, 1918.

The San Jose Branch was opened for traffic in 1921.

The Sacramento Northern Railway, another interurban line, was purchased in 1921. Construction of the SN actually began in 1905 from Chico to Oroville and was originally named the Northern Electric. The NE was renamed the Sacramento Northern in 1918. Meanwhile, still another electric interurban had been built between Oakland and Sacramento, the Oakland and Antioch. Later the name was changed to the Oakland, Antioch and Eastern. (11)

As with all the interurban lines. The OA&E eventually went into receivership and was reorganized in 1920 as the San Francisco - Sacramento Railroad. It was also known as the Sacramento Short Line. The WP purchased the railroad in February, 1927. Two years later, the WP merged the two electric lines with the Sacramento Northern being the surviving name. Passenger service was discontinued in 1941 and the roads were dieselized in April, 1945. The SN operated independently on approximately 336 miles of track between Concord and Chico, California. (12) (See Chapter 2)

All of the railroads passed into the hands of the United States Railroad Administration in 1918. The Western Pacific was no exception, and the arrangement continued for nearly

The company maintained and operated a two track diesel house at Elko, Nevada. The date is August 13, 1983, and Union Pacific power can be seen to the right of this compact and effective facility. (Bob Larson)

This photo illustrates the new yard tracks and new yard office at Elko, Nevada in August, 1983. The philosophy of WP maintenance and rebuilding continued under the UP banner. (Bob Larson)

two years. During that time, the SP and the WP worked out an agreement to pair their track operations between Weso and Alazon in Nevada. Also under the USRA, an arrangement was made to balance the traffic on the WP and SP main lines. In this case, the SP had a heavier eastbound traffic than westbound, while the WP had lighter eastbound traffic. It was also decided that the WP would be used as far as possible for business between the coast and Salt Lake City in order to avoid the hauling of freight through Ogden to get to or from Salt Lake City. Western Pacific freight was also routed via the SP around San Francisco through the use of the SP's Dumbarten Bridge. This eliminated the use of WP boats on the bay. (13)

After 1920, when the railroads were returned to private operation, the WP had the task of rebuilding their railroad and continuing the objectives and goals prior to the USRA and World War I. In 1923, the Calpine Branch was opened to traffic in the Feather River Canyon. This particular line was abandoned in 1940.

In 1924 in an economy move, the WP and the SP resumed the paired track agreement mentioned previously.

Arthur Curtiss James acquired control of the WP in 1926. James also had large holdings in the Great Northern, Northern Pacific and the Burlington Route. Under James' direction, the President Harry M. Adams, the WP was completely rebuilt. At the same time, the Alameda Belt Line was purchased by the WP and the Santa Fe from the City of Alameda. And this was not the end of the WP's expansion and economic changes.

The company acquired 33% interest in the Central California Traction Company, a 53 mile railroad that connected Sacramento with Stockton on January 1, 1928. The same

year, the Terminous Branch including a dock and warehouse was opened to serve the California "Delta" area growers and shippers. This line was closed in 1964. (14)

One of the many problems the railroads had to face was the lack of courtesy among train and station crews toward the public. Many of the western railroads recognized this problem early, and set out to solve with positive action rather than the "can't do it" approach. The WP, along with the Great Northern and the Baltimore and Ohio (although not at the same time), was one of the first railroads to establish a courtesy program for train and station employees and supervisors, and for other personnel that came in contact with the traveling and shipping public. "You are the company" was the basic theme of these programs. The WP's program was very successful and the company was noted for its positive approach with customers and the general public.

The reader will recall that A. C. James controlled the WP and was a substantial stockholder in the Great Northern Railway. Plans were formulated for the construction of a GN-WP link in northern California. At the same time, the WP had two other equally ambitious plans. In early 1928, the WP incorporated the Western Pacific California Railroad with a capital of $15 million to build 174 miles of railroad for $13,500,000. Initial plans called for a 25 mile line from San Francisco to Redwood City, eventually to be connected with the main line at Niles giving a direct all rail route to San Francisco. This line would have cost $3,700,000. The second plan called for a 138 mile extension from Niles Garden on the main line to Kings River south of Fresno. This line would have cost $8,500,000 to build and was ultimately projected to be constructed all the way to Bakersfield. (15)

Neither of these plans ever went beyond the drawing board stage. The SP testified in both cases they served the area and that new construction would have been a duplication of services.

The Northern California route was, and is, a different story. On January 29, 1929, the final decision to build the GN-WP link was made at a conference at San Francisco with Ralph Budd, President of the GN; H. M. Adams, President of the WP, and Chairman Arthur Curtiss James. (16) On June 20, 1930, the ICC approved the plan as set forth by the Great Northern and the Western Pacific.

It is interesting to note that James, who was the controlling stockholder and Chairman of the WP, and the largest individual stockholder of the GN, was also a large stockholder of the Southern Pacific. The new WP extension with the GN would directly compete with the SP. Yet it was James who pushed through the Bieber project and thereby fulfilled the long cherished dream of the Great Northern's Jim Hill of establishing another link between California and the Pacific Northwest. The caliber of James was shown by the fact that immediately after participating in the opening of the seven mile long Cascade tunnel on the GN in January, 1929, he boarded his car to go to San Francisco to finalize plans for the joint railroad extension. A large portion of the money expended by the Western Pacific was advanced by James personally. (17) He was therefore the most logical selection to drive the gold spike. The gold spike, by the way, was a gift of the Oroville, California Chamber of Commerce. It contained gold mined in five different ways: panned, placer mined, from tunnels in ancient river beds, from a quartz mine, and from a gold dredge. According to RAILWAY AGE, he declined the honor at first but accepted when it was made clear to him that his connection with the two railroads made him the man for the event. He cheerfully took off his coat and said, "Let me have the maul and I will hit the spike as often as I can." (18) There was a total of six trainloads of quests in the temporary grandstand that faced the speaker's platform across the track where one rail was still missing. It was a cold afternoon that November 10, 1931 with a few flakes of snow falling. The event included music and speeches by railroad officials and other people. Then the track gang carried the last rail to its place and drove all the spikes but one with their pneumatic hammers. Then as described above, Arthur C. James drove the gold spike to mark the completion of the GN-WP extension that became known as the "Inside Gateway." Then two locomotives, Western Pacific No. 204, and Great Northern No. 3351 drew slowly together until H. M. Adams and Ralph Budd, respective presidents of the two lines, standing on the pilots could clasp hands. Then the engines were speedily backed away for traffic was already waiting to use the new railroad. A 150 car freight train sped south between the grandstand and the speaker's platform. As the caboose slid by, a snow storm moved in and the crowd tore down the grandstand and built a bonfire to keep warm until their special trains backed in. A dream had come true. A new railroad line had been born. (19)

As mentioned previously, the route via Bieber makes up a fast through freight line running just east of the Sierras and the Cascade mountains linking California and the North Pacific Coast. Although the line is a north-south artery, the route was invaluable to the GN and the WP in extending the usefulness of the transcontinental east-west routes. Opening the Bieber line enabled the GN to solicit transcontinental business to and from central and even southern California over a line that was intimately linked with its own transcontinental line, and with a substantial broadening of the extent and geographical and commodity range of through rates, diversions and reconsignment privileges. It is interesting to note that the ICC, in approving the line, noticed that the territory service by the Great Northern and its connections from Eastern Washington to Minnesota and Southern Canada, the consumption of California perishables

We must zip back in time for a moment to 1958. This overhead view shows the Portola Yard with switch shanty, old depot and old freight house. The Portola Yard portrays the smaller, but very important intermediate yards that could be found on all transcontinental lines throughout North America. It was these facilities that made many of the small intermediate towns into important centers - for education, transportation, and just plain healthful living with a sense of community. Portola, California is such a town. (Bob Larson)

was far below the average for the country as a whole. Similarly, the extension put the WP in a more favorable position to handle business to and from the Pacific Northwest over its transcontinental route. (20) Of all the investments made by the Western Pacific, the "Inside Gateway" was the most rewarding.

The Western Pacific went through the next two decades (1931 - 1951) that were radically different. The first ten years were spent with the Depression that caused the WP to fail financially for the second time in its history. A plan by the Reconstruction Finance Corporation called for the reorganization and the railroad was rebuilt from the rails up. Because of the rebuilding, the railroad was ready to face the Second World War. The company was in excellent shape, and performed well during those war years. Chapter 7 describes the freight services and the tonnages handled during those two decades.

Frederick B. Whitman became president of the Western Pacific on July 1, 1947, succeeding Mr. H. A. Mitchell, who retired. Peace time operations were settling in to a normal scheme of things and thoughts turned from the war to other things. The railroad would soon be 40 years old.

The company celebrated its anniversary with the driving of a ruby spike on Spanish Creek Bridge near Keddie, California, where the original last spike was driven in 1909. Taking part in the cel-

ebration were the California Zephyr, the old ten wheeler No. 94, which hauled the first train down the Feather River Canyon, and the wood burning "Jupiter." The ruby spike was driven, appropriately, by Lenord diTomasso, who was the foreman who hammered the last spike to open the Feather River Route on November 1, 1909. Whistles of the two steam engines, and the Zephyr's air horn blended with the music from various school bands located in the canyon below. A large crowd watched the ceremony from the Feather River highway, which had been blocked off for the celebration. Among the many people who were present included: Senator William F. Knowband, F. B. Whitman, and H. A. Mitchell. (21) One could say it was a celebration that was 40 years late.

It could be said that Mr. Whitman was one of the more dynamic railroad presidents in the United States. He put into practice several innovations that were and are certainly deserving of being put into practice in all types of organiza-

Greenville, California was located on the former Fourth Subdivision of the Western Division on the Northern California Extension to Bieber. The train order signals are displaying "stop" for orders in both directions, as detouring Southern Pacific No. 14, Amtrak's Starlight, moves through a cross-over on to the main line. The date of this detour operation is December 16, 1973. Greenville as of the late 1980s was located on the Bieber Subdivision of the Feather River Division. (Bob Larson)

tions and companies today. One such practice by Mr. Whitman was to invite the entire personnel of the railroad to have dinner with him. In 1950, the number of employees on the WP was around 5000. It was Mr. Whitman's intention to have dinner at various locations on the railroad so that he could personally tell the employees of his plans for the future development of the railroad. Seventeen separate parties were held at various locations which brought Mr. Whitman into personal contact with the entire staff. Special trains took groups of employees to towns where adequate dining facilities existed, and railroad dining cars provided for the repast in isolated areas. (22)

It so happened in 1950, when Mr. Whitman was con-

The public was also invited to the festivities that marked the 50th year of organization. The WP set up a display of old and new railroad equipment at the Sacramento depot. Included was a train of the 1870s, a diesel locomotive, a California Zephyr coach, a compartmentizer box car, and the Military Blood Procurement car, the Charles O. Sweetwood, which the railroad used for blood collections in rural areas where other blood donor facilities were not available. The company also provided guided tours of the Traffic Control System, otherwise known as Centralized Traffic Control or CTC. (25)

During the two decades following World War II, the Western Pacific steadily and consistently up graded the rail-

It is 1958, and the surrounding territory will be under water in the years to come. This is the location of the then proposed Oroville Dam site on the "Feather River" which was marked by a "Feather" sign. (Bob Larson)

ducting these meetings, the railroad brotherhoods were in daily negotiations with the company. Mr. Whitman had personally invited all of the general chairmen of the various brotherhoods to accompany him on the entire trip. When the men pointed out that negotiations were underway and that their presence was required in San Francisco, Mr. Whitman ordered another business car added to the train and suggested that negotiations be continued en route. The invitation was accepted. (23)

The Western Pacific celebrated the 50th Anniversary of the company's INCORPORATION in 1953. A special cachet was issued with its cancellation by the San Francisco's post office on the March 3rd date. Philatelists were invited to send a self-addressed stamped envelope to the WP's Public Relations Department before February 27th. The cachet was then affixed and the post office cancelled the envelope for mailing on the celebration date. (24)

road. In fact, it could be said that the WP was exceptionally well maintained. An example of such improvements was the new Feather River Canyon tunnel opened in 1957. The company spent $2 million constructing the tunnel in an area where there were frequent land and mud slides. Eventually the tunnel paid for itself with the elimination of delays to trains and costs for clearing the track after a slide, not to mention repair costs.

The last major change in WP trackage came in 1962. At that time train service was begun over a new $40 million 23 mile line change in northern California. The change was carried out to replace nearly 27 miles of main line in the Feather River Canyon. The reason for the relocation was the construction of the Oroville Dam, which inundated the old main line. The new line departed from the old line at a point a few hundred feet north of the Oroville depot location, which was four miles down stream from the dam site. It then makes a wide swing to the west before turning north and rejoining the existing line along the North Fork of the Feather River. The territory is mountainous and sparsely populated. It is cut by several rivers and streams flowing in deep valleys and gorges. The specifications for the new section of track called for a maximum of 1% compensated grade, and maximum curvature of 4 degrees, 30 minutes. In order to hold to these requirements, it was necessary to build a number of tunnels and high bridges plus deep cuts, high fills and several meandering curves of the "kidney" variety. (26)

Mr. Whitman retired in 1965 and was replaced by Mr. M. M. Christy, who in turn was replaced by Mr. A. E. Perlman in late 1970. After two years of losses, the WP turned a profit of $3.9 million in 1971. As of December, 1972, the WP operated 1,246 miles of main line track plus 472 miles of branch line trackage including the Sacramento Northern and Tidewater Southern Railways. The railroad was actively working to encourage industry to locate near WP trackage.

The railroad was alive and well in the early 1970s, and continued to make progress. It did this feat against strong competitive transportation companies and against nature itself. The land itself had played a major role with the WP's challenges over the decades of operation. The railroad's two divisions had two completely different operating environments.

The climate and the various conditions of an area can and does have an impact on train operations. The Western Pacific's main line traversed through two distinct areas. On the west end, the California mountains required helper service, while the east end through the Nevada Desert has high winds and sand problems.

The mountain areas were (and are) subject to heavy rain fall, which would cause slides and washouts. The tunnel recently mentioned had to be built for just those reasons. In the winter - well that means "snow time!" The WP maintained a fleet of rotary snow plows and could call upon various pieces of maintenance of way equipment for additional help, such as dirt dozers and Jordon Spreaders, which are equipped with pilot plows. Although winter can be and is beautiful, it means a lot of hard work from November to April.

Despite the fact that the main line has mountain grades of no more than 1%, the trains still required helper engines. In this case, the WP usually ran three to six units on the head-end of the train, with the two helper units about two thirds of the way back in the train. The helper districts were located in the Feather River Canyon, and also on the "Inside Gateway." The Western Division held many challenges along with its great beauty.

In contrast, the Eastern Division was almost like a dif-

The scenery on the Western Division was (is) nothing less than spectacular. "Out of the Tunnel and on to the Bridge" is just was happens between Tunnels 31 and 32. This photo was taken in 1957 by Bob Larson.

Truly a land mark on the WP is the Keddie Wye, with its curved steel deck viaducts. The Northern California Extension heads off to the left over Spanish Creek. (Bob Larson Collection)

ferent railroad. According to Mr. H. J. Beam, the former Division Superintendent of the Eastern Division at Elko, Nevada; during the early years of the railroad, the steam power had to haul auxiliary water tenders. This was necessary because of a lack of fresh water for the 72 miles on the east end of the division. It was not uncommon between 1910 and 1915 for the steam power to run out of fuel and water before they reached the end of that desert stretch. It also happened in those early days that during high wind storms across the desert, that the locomotive fireman would desert his post after the engine ran out of fuel. He would literally flag down the first passenger train that would came along.

The WP constructed a 90,000 gallon reservoir at a midway point in the desert in order to eliminate the problem of running out of water. This also enabled the railroad to discontinue the auxiliary water car.

During the days of steam, the desert winds would often require reductions of freight train tonnage in order to maintain time schedules of the faster freights. The high winds also caused the problem of drifting sand, and this is still a problem in the area. The sand storms not only reduced visibility, but would also get into the engine cabs and other parts of the locomotives as well as the freight car journal boxes. This in turn caused hot boxes. Also if sand gets into the traction motors on diesel power, it causes a loss of power. Another problem during the days of steam was the distribution of water tank cars to various locations that would run short sooner than expected. The freight trains had the job of picking up and setting out these water cars at various stations.

For another view of this spectacular bridge - from the locomotive cab, we have Bob Larson to thank for this shot on June 13, 1963 when they were putting the rails back on the Northern California Extension.

As the WP moved into the 1970s with A. E. Perlman, the company began a series of twists and turns that would take it through "railroad to holding company and back to railroad" with a variety of activities. Some of these were minor, and some were major. For example, the Financial Analysts Federation cited the WP for excellence in corporate reporting in early 1971. (27) On the other hand, when the WP wished to issue $6 million in short term notes, the ICC declared that it could only do so if the proceeds were used only for railroad working capital. It banned any uses for dividends or advances to affiliated companies. It was the first time in history that the ICC ever did this. (28)

Perlman became Chairman of the Board and Chief Executive Officer and Robert G. Flannery became President in late 1972. (29) Flannery would be part of the railroad operations and planning for the next decade.

The railroad merger picture played a major role in the WP's future. The Burlington Northern was assembled in 1970, and the WP became a likely candidate for many carriers, with stock having been purchased by such lines as the Southern Pacific and the former Great Northern. However, the process from the holding company to the Union Pacific System is one of the more interesting stories of railroad economic history and development during the 1970s and 80s and later.

The managers of the Western Pacific openly stated that the WP was first and foremost a "railroad." The plan included a clear strategy for maintaining and improving its position until the restructuring took place. Frank Malone, Associate Editor of RAILWAY AGE, wrote a key article in the November 12, 1979 issue explaining this process.

The WP launched a new logo in October, 1979 that symbolized the WP's strength as the Feather River Route. The new logo was a result of the sale of the railroad to Newrail Company, Inc., a corporation formed by the railroad's management expressly to purchase the property from the parent Western Pacific Industries. The reader may recall that the WPI itself had been formed from the railroad during the period 1971-1972.

Another characteristic that adds hard work and romance to the soul are the many bridges, snow sheds and rock slide fences along the WP's main line. This scene is near Pulga on the former Third Subdivision of the Western Division. (Bob Larson, June 15, 1963)

Keddie Yard played an important role in the train operations north to Bieber. A train of ballast cars occupies the yard in this July, 1958 photo by Bob Larson.

Newrail paid WPI $14 million, which was generated through issuance of 1.4 million Class A common shares sold at $10 per share, and assumed the railroad's liabilities of $114 million. With the completion of the sale, the company name was changed to Western Pacific Railroad Company, and the name Newrail ceased to exist.

The Western Pacific was a publically owned railroad that was controlled by management through the device of Class B common stock. Holders of the Class B stock, which was held only by the top seven offices of the company had the right to appoint the majority of the Western Pacific board for the first five years.

The Chicago and North Western and the Union Pacific Railroads each purchased approximately 10% of the WP Class A stock, which was publicly traded over the counter, and then later on the American Stock Exchange.

President Flannery saw the WP as an essential element in a single line West Coast - Chicago system. At the time of Malone's article, Flannery felt that the UP would indeed need the WP in face of the Southern Pacific's proposed purchase of the Rock Island line from Santa Rosa, New Mexico to St. Louis, Missouri. (30)

The purchase of the Rock Island's Tucumcari line convinced the UP that the WP was the only way to go. It began buy out talks with the WP, and at the same time began serious discussions with the Missouri Pacific. (31)

These negotiations ultimately led to the merger of the Western Pacific into the Union Pacific, along with the Missouri Pacific. The merger brought on a new set of operations, which are briefly covered in the Epilogue. Meanwhile, the remainder of this book is devoted to the WP freight and passenger train operations.

Endnotes:

1. John K. Kelly, WESTERN PACIFIC, San Francisco, California: The Western Pacific Railroad Company, 1972, p. 1.
2. Kelly, p. 2.
3. Kelly, p. 2.
4. Kelly, p. 2.
5. Kelly, p. 2.
6. Kelly, p. 6.
7. RAILWAY AGE GAZETTE, April 15, 1910, p. 1002.
8. RAILWAY AGE GAZETTE, 1915, p. 998.
9. Kelly, p. 5.
10. Kelly, p. 5.
11. Kelly, p. 5.
12. Kelly, p. 5.
13. RAILWAY AGE GAZETTE, 1915, p. 187 and 829.
14. Kelly, p. 6.

The following endnotes from 15 to 29 are from RAILWAY AGE, Dates shown:

15. Feb. 23, 1929, p. 469.
16. Feb. 23, 1929, p. 469.
17, 18, 19 and 20. Jan. 7, 1952, p. 52.
21. November 26, 1949, p. 975.
22 and 23. May 13, 1950, p. 928.
24 and 25. March 16, 1953, p. 13.
26. November, 1962, p. 14.
27. March 29, 1971, p. 8.
28. March 8, 1971, p. 15.
29. October 30, 1972, p. 8
30. Frank Malone, "A Key Piece in the Western Pacific," RAILWAY AGE, November 12, 1979, p. 16.
31. Gus Welty, "UP/MP/WP: A Whole Greater Than the Sum of the Parts," RAILWAY AGE, April 27, 1981, p. 20.

Chapter 2

WESTERN PACIFIC SUBSIDIARIES

Virtually all major railroad companies owned one or more subsidiaries and this was the case for the Western Pacific. Since the carrier played a major role in transcontinental traffic, it played the part of a much larger railroad than one might think in terms of a carrier with less than 1500 route miles. The purpose of this chapter is to briefly review the various subsidiaries of the WP.

Sacramento Northern Railway

The largest of the various subsidiaries was the SN. Originally an electric interurban line, the company ultimately operated 336 miles of track between Concord and Chico, California; and was an important feeder for the WP. Motive power ranged from neat little electric locomotives to F3s and GP9 diesel electrics. The company operated some fairly good sized trains and utilized a certain amount of hand-me-down equipment, such as cabooses and other equipment for its operations.

The Tidewater Southern

The Tidewater Southern extended from Stockton in a southerly direction to Ortega, Modesto, Hatch and Turlock, a distance of 47.9 miles. As with the Sacramento Northern, the company provided the WP with a valuable traffic base serving manufacturing, farming and wine producing areas.

The Sacramento Northern was quite well known for its electric interurban passenger service. Combine 1005, with its pantograph raised to the overhead catenary, leads a trailer on a rail fan special at Pittsburg, California on December 13, 1957. (Bob Larson)

Other subsidiaries of the company included the following railroads or companies:

Name:	Percentage Owned:
Salt Lake City Union Depot and Railroad	50.0
Alameda Belt Line	50.0
Central California Traction Company	50.0
Pullman Company	.42
Oakland Terminal Railway	50.0
Fruit Growers Express	1.05

A close up view of the combine 1014 when in passenger service at Concord, California in February, 1940. The combine carried the "Railway Express Agency" diamond insignia, and the large door provided entry for the motorman as well as packages. The sad part of all this is the Sacramento Northern electric passenger services were discarded as nothing but obsolete past history. The passenger routes are now needed again to provide a balanced public transportation system in this area. As a side note, California in the 21st Century is now leading North America in the creation of new passenger train services. (Bob Larson Collection)

Electric freight motor No. 430 carried both the pantograph and the trolley pole for electrical pick-up. The 430's portrait was taken in service at Marysville in 1942. The hooded headlights, on each hood, were designed to reduce as much light as possible. It was World War II with fear of attacks on the west coast of the U.S. For that reason, night had to be as dark as possible. (Bob Larson)

It is December 31, 1956, and SN 652 has lost its pantograph. The unit is at the end of its days here at the WP shops in Sacramento. The little electric displays the last lettering, numbering, and striping scheme of the final days of Sacramento Northern electric operations. (Bob Larson)

The Sacramento Northern took on more of a look as an "Intercity Terminal Railroad" with dieselization. SN power, such as the SW-1 No. 401 (ex-WP 501) wore the WP colors of silver and orange. The unit, built in 1939, was already 33 years old when its portrait was taken in action at Yuba City in October, 1972. (Bob Larson)

A bit of the "interurban" look was retained through the use of a General Electric 44 ton, center cab switch engine, not much unlike the design of the earlier electrics. The 146 is laying over at Walnut Creek, California with its wooden caboose. (Photo by T. Gray, July, 1958, Bob Larson Collection)

Sacramento Northern 301 literally matches WP 801D (with the exception of the silver pilot and trucks), and the two present a team approach with matching colors, but with different road names. Such combinations added class as well as a strong hint of cooperative and team efforts between railroads, even though the SN was a subsidiary of the WP. The two units are handling a SN detour train at Stockton in June, 1958. (Bob Larson)

The appearance of heavy duty railroading took a leap forward with the purchase of ex- New York, Ontario and Western F-3s. In this case, the 301 and 302 show off their WP look with the orange and silver paint scheme. Coupled to a wooden caboose, the pair are ready for any and all freight service on the SN.

(NYO&W No. 501, Sacramento, August 6, 1957, Bob Larson)
(SN 301 and 302, Stockton, California, 1957, Bob Larson)

For our final photo of the SN, GP-7 No. 712 wears green and orange WP colors at Yuba City, California. It is March 9, 1984, and such scenes will soon be part of history. (Bob Larson)

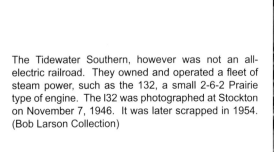

The Tidewater Southern, however was not an all-electric railroad. They owned and operated a fleet of steam power, such as the 132, a small 2-6-2 Prairie type of engine. The I32 was photographed at Stockton on November 7, 1946. It was later scrapped in 1954. (Bob Larson Collection)

The Tidewater Southern too operated a freight service behind electric motive power, and in this case, with only one trolley pole for electrical pick-up. No. 100 was photographed at Modesto, California in 1944. (Bob Larson Collection)

The Tidewater Southern No 735 was a General Electric 44 ton switcher. The unit also reflected its Western Pacific heritage by its silver and orange colors. The 735 is shown here in service at Turlock, California on what later became the Tidewater Southern Subdivision of the WP's Feather River Division. (November, 1957, Bob Larson)

TS 743 also carried the WP colors. (November 6, 1956, Bob Larson)

Tidewater Southern Alco S-2s, wearing WP colors, placed the railroad more closely to its real purpose: switching services, pick-up and deliveries, and short over-the-road train operations. These two units, the 744 and 745, ultimately became the WP's second 554 and 552 respectively. The two units were painted orange when photographed in July, 1967 at Stockton, California. (Bob Larson)

Tidewater Southern's Alco RS-1 No. 747, began life as Spokane International's 205, and then Union Pacific's 1216, and it finally went to the TS. The unit was, along with its sister unit 746, the largest and heaviest power ever owned by the TS. The 746 and 747 wore their UP colors with TS lettering for a few months as illustrated here. The units were painted in the WP green in 1972. In a sense, the 747 in the UP color scheme was pre-cognitive of a decade later when the Union Pacific acquired the WP. (Bob Larson)

For all appearances, it would look as though this were a Western Pacific cab hop. However, it is a Tidewater Southern train at Modesto, California running east to Turlock on the TS main line between Stockton Yard and Turlock. The GP9 No. 725 and caboose were photographed in action on April 14, 1975. (Bob Larson)

Chapter 3

FLYERS, LOCALS and PASSENGER EXTRAS

What many people consider to be the Golden Era of railroading began on August 22, 1910 for the newly completed Western Pacific Railroad. The first passenger train arrived in Oakland with a large celebration. The Oakland depot was dedicated and a parade escorted the first passengers to a dinner at one of the local country clubs. Everyone was happy not only because of the new passenger service to and from the east, but it broke the monopoly of the Southern Pacific System between California and Utah. (1)

The passenger train of 1910, named the Overland Express, was not a big train by any standard. It was essentially a long distance local train between Oakland and Salt Lake City. The running time east bound was 38 hours, while its west bound counter-part made the trip in 36 hours, 29 minutes. The consist of the express in those early days was as follows:

```
1 Combine
1 Coach
1 Tourist Sleeping Car
1 Dining Car (Leased from the Rio Grande)
1 First Class Sleeping Car
1 Buffet Library Observation Car
```

Motive power for the "Express" was a "Ten Wheeler." The WP owned 35 such locomotives (71 to 106), all of which were constructed by Alco in 1908 and 1909. These class TP-29s were limited to 780 tons, which was approximately 10 cars, westward from Wendover to Shafter on the Eastern Division, and 910 tons westward on the First Subdivision of the Western Division. Therefore, since the size of the trains at that time were relatively short, the ten wheelers were ample power.

It is interesting to note that the WP purchased 35 passenger locomotives, even though there was to be only one passenger train each way daily. However, with the time schedule of the time, all of the locomotives were utilized. If one considers that locomotives were changed at subdivision points and the fact that five sets of trains were required to maintain the daily service, 30 locomotives were constantly in use or being serviced at one of the six subdivision points. The other five were maintained for substitute and/or extra service.

The Western Pacific purchased very few passenger cars during the early years. In fact, even by 1917, the company owned but five head-end cars, one combination car and one business car. Nearly all of the passenger equipment operating on the WP was leased from the Rio Grande with the

Western Pacific's 484 was part of an earlier order with Southern Pacific power. The WP's 4-8-4's carried the streamlined design, but did not have any streamliner color schemes, such as found with the SP power. The 484 here was photographed at Salt Lake City on July 26, 1946 with the first section of the Exposition Flyer. Note the green flags indicating a following section on the same train schedule. In 1945 and 46, the WP handled a substantial number of military personnel returning from duty with the end of the war. The WP's streamlined Northerns, such as the 484, were spectacular pieces of power and provided a valuable and needed service. (Robert Kennedy, Collection of Jay Williams, Big Four Graphics)

The Feather River Express, with a short four car consist, rolls through Sacramento behind Ten Wheeler No. 83 in July, 1942. Only a wisp of smoke comes from the stack as the steamer makes easy work of the train which does not have a troop movement on this beautiful July day. (Harold K. Vollrath Collection)

exception of the Pullman sleeping cars.

The WP's single passenger train continued to operate as a local train until 1915. Basically, the passenger business had been relatively disappointing. The company carried 256,099 passengers in 1912. By 1915, it had dropped to 233,141.

The Panama Pacific Exposition opened in San Francisco in 1915. This provided a source for new passenger business and the WP spruced up the local by giving it a new name, the Pacific Express. (2) However, the train continued to remain a local service with through car service in conjunction with the Rio Grande and the Burlington railroads. The WP continued to lease passenger equipment from the Rio Grande, in fact, a total of 20 coaches, 20 baggage cars, and 8 dining cars. This equipment carried the name "Western Pacific" in the letter board with Rio Grande sub lettering in the corner. This arrangement continued until 1923.

Passenger patronage just didn't seem to have any zip in it all. Except for World War I, patronage continued to slide from the very beginning. In 1922, the total number of passengers was 201,623. The following year it did increase to 220,764 passengers. At the same time, the WP returned the lease equipment to the Rio Grande and purchased 20 coaches and 8 dining cars. It was the largest passenger equipment purchase ever made by the WP exceeding even that of the California Zephyr purchase in 1947. The company also purchased one business car in 1920 and two motor cars in 1922. The motor cars provided service on the San Jose branch line.

In 1924 and 1925, the company added two more baggage cars and one combination car to the roster, which stood as follows as of December 31, 1925:

Head-end cars	25
Combination cars	2
Motor Cars	2
Coaches	20
Dining Cars	8
Business Cars	2

Exciting things did not really begin to happen to Western Pacific passenger service until the late 1920s. The Scenic Limited had been operating for quite some time and on June 9, 1929, the company placed the train on a 27 hour schedule between Salt Lake City and the coast. This was a reduction of 1 hours and 15 minutes according to the 1929 volume of RAILWAY AGE. At the same time, the Pacific Express' running time was reduced from 33 hours, 45 minutes to 33 hours, 15 minutes. Although passenger patronage continued to drop, 157, 436 in 1928, the company embarked on a program to improve service.

First of all, the company purchased four coach-diners and one business car in 1928. The following year, another business car was added along with 25 express refers from General American Tank Car Company. This equipment was acquired for strawberry and other perishable shipments that

It is April, 1946, and first 39, the Exposition Flyer is arriving at Oakland, California. WP's 179 is carrying green flags indicating the following section. The consist on this morning continues to reflect heavy military personnel movements as two troop sleepers are cut in behind the baggage cars, and ahead of the coaches. The Exposition Flyer was the WP's most successful passenger train until the advent of the "California Zephyr." (Harold K. Vollrath Collection)

were shipped via Railway Express Agency on the Western Pacific.

In addition to the new and expanded equipment roster, the railroad improved service again on January 4, 1931. The number of passengers carried in 1930 had dropped to 115,787. The company was determined to reverse the trend by positive action instead of discontinuing service. According to the January 24, 1931 issue of RAILWAY AGE, the schedule of the Scenic Limited was cut a full 11 hours, 15 minutes between the west coast and Chicago, and 8 hours, 30 minutes between the coast and St. Louis. The Pacific Express' schedule was reduced by 6 hours, 15 minutes between Oakland and Salt Lake City.

Not only was train service speeded up on the four regular trains in operation at that time, but a new train was placed in service between Oakland and Reno, Nevada. The entire purpose of the new train was to relieve the Pacific Express from local work. The new train made all stops between Oakland and Reno and provided over-night service between the two points. The new train, known as the Feather River Express, carried a 12 Section, 1 Drawing Room sleeping car between Oakland and Portola along with dining car service. Coaches operated between all points. Although the January 4, 1931 time table is not entirely clear, it is believed that two of the four coach diners purchased in 1928 were operated on trains 5 and 6, one for each set of equipment.

At the same time, the Scenic Limited, trains 1 and 2, carried two 12 Section, 1 Drawing Room sleepers for Denver, a 10 Section Observation

Sleeper between the coast and Salt Lake City, coaches and a dining car. The through sleeping cars operated via the Rio Grande.

Trains 3 and 4, the Pacific Express, carried a 10 Section, 2 Compartment, 1 Drawing Room sleeper for Chicago and a similar car for St. Louis. This through car service operated via the Rio Grande, Burlington and the Missouri Pacific railroads. Coach and dining car service was also provided.

Another improvement came on May 18, 1931 when through sleeping car service between Chicago and the West Coast was established on the WP-D&RGW's Scenic Limited, and the Burlington's Aristocrat. (3)

This photo of train 39 illustrates the appeal of mixed streamlined and standard equipment in the same train. In this case, the newly arriving California Zephyr domes have created a "Domeliner" out of the Exposition Flyer in a "classic" sense. The train was photographed east of Portola approaching Arnold Loop on the Third Subdivision of the old Western Division of the WP. (Frank McKinlay, Rail Photo Service, Author's Collection)

The ultimate in travel for the Exposition Flyer came when newly delivered "California Zephyr" dome coaches were placed in service on trains 39 and 40. The "Flyer" was running in the pre-CZ days with a mixture of silver CZ equipment and green Western Pacific, Rio Grande and Burlington passenger equipment. Three Western Pacific F units are powering this hybrid train to wet the appetites of people looking forward to "Domeliner" travel. (Photo by B. F. Cutler, Rail Photo Service, Author's Collection)

Except for the retirement of 1 combination car in 1937, the WP's passenger car roster remained stable throughout the Depression. The express refers, and coach diners remained in operation until 1939. In 1934, the WP air conditioned 10 of the cars operated on the Scenic Limited. This included the three lounge observations, three sleeping cars, and four of the company's eight dining cars. A steam ejector apparatus was used for the air conditioning of the dining cars. (4)

Train schedules were also adjusted in 1934. The Scenic Limited was sped up by 1 hour and five minutes between Salt Lake City and the coast. (5) The adjustment took place on June 17th, when the Denver and Rio Grande Western Railroad completed the Dotsero cut-off in Colorado. This cut-off saved 175 miles on the D&RGW's Denver - Salt Lake City route. (6) It should be mentioned at this point that the Pacific Express was discontinued in 1933 when passenger patronage hit an all time low of 44,574. From that time, except for 1938, patronage would continue to grow and did so until after World War II.

During the summer of 1938, another adjustment altered the schedule of the Scenic Limited. Previous to this time, the schedule of the train sent it through the Feather River Canyon at night. As of June 12th, the train ran through the Canyon in daylight. (7)

Part of this adjustment was the planning for the new transcontinental train service by the Western Pacific, Rio Grande and Burlington railroads. Another adjustment and speed up took place in early 1939. This time, the schedule between Chicago and the coast was 57 hours westbound, and 60 hours eastbound. (8) By the end of March, 1939, the Chicago and North Western, Union Pacific and Southern Pacific railroads objected to the new schedule based on a gentlemen's agreement among the transcontinental roads that all trains on schedules of less than 60 hours would be "Extra Fare" trains. As a result of the discussions, the CB&Q, Rio Grande and WP adjusted the schedule of the westbound to 59 hours, 55 minutes. This schedule was exactly the same as the C&NW-UP-SP San Francisco Challenger, an economy tourist sleeper and coach train between Chicago and the West Coast. (9)

Meanwhile, the Burlington, Rio Grande and the WP fi-nalized plans for a deluxe train between Chicago and San Francisco. A general announcement regarding the new train was made in the early part of 1939. The train, to be known as the Exposition Flyer, was to be placed in service on June 10th and would be a summer only operation.

The new Exposition Flyer was dedicated with inaugural ceremonies at Chicago including a Christening with a mixture of waters from San Francisco Bay, the Feather River Canyon, Great Salt Lake, the Colorado, Missouri, and Mississippi Rivers and Lake Michigan. Music was provided by the Aurora, Illinois high school band with a series of brief addresses by Albert Cotsworth, Passenger Traffic Manager for the Burlington; Hugh Scofield, Passenger Traffic Manager for the Rio Grande; and Joseph Wheeler, General Passenger Agent for the WP. Five hostess nurses, who were part of the train personnel, impersonated Miss Treasure Island, Miss Feather River, Miss Salt Lake City, Miss Denver, and Miss Chicago. (10)

The Western Pacific powered the Exposition Flyer with the steam generator equipped F-3 motive power from Electro-Motive. This photo is literally a prelude to the eventual motive power to be part of the California Zephyr pool. (Jay Williams Collection, Big Four Graphics)

The new train service began June 10, 1939, and demand for accommodations on the Flyer was so great that six extra sleepers and an extra dining cars were added to handle the overflow business. As a result of this extra business, train No. 9, which departed at 10:30 a.m. (Five hours and 30 minutes ahead of the Flyer) and handled the head-end business and local passenger traffic for the Exposition Flyer between Chicago and Ottumwa, Iowa; operated as a second section to Oakland west of Ottumwa on the first day of operation.

Prior to World War II, train 9 was combined with the Flyer, No. 39, at Ottumwa. Patronage continued its high initial surge, and similar two section operations were required on June 13 and the 15th. On June 17 and 18, business was even heavier and the Flyer departed Chicago in two sections. Train 9 was then combined with "Second No. 39" at Ottumwa. The standard operating procedure for extra section running usually found the first section as an "All-Pullman" train. (11) The company was most happy with the early reception of the Exposition Flyer.

The train was so popular that Western Pacific passenger business jumped nearly 33% from 1938 to 1939. The 1938 figure was 50,516 passengers traveling 22,987,531 WP passenger miles. As of December 31, 1939, the twelve month figure was 75,161 with 43,484,247 WP passenger miles. It was the highest figure since 1931, and was actually accomplished with the fewest number of trains. The Pacific Express had been gone since 1933. The Feather River Express had been cut back from its Reno destination to Portola. The train was replaced by a mixed train on the branch to Reno. This cut back meant that there was but one train each way east of Portola.

A good deal of the Flyer's popularity was due to the services it offered. Even though the train was basically a Chicago - Oakland train, it carried a number of cars to and from the West Coast for other major Mid-western cities. The basic equipment and routings for the Exposition Flyer in 1939 was as follows: (12)

Equipment	Routing
Head-end cars (2 or more)	Chicago - Oakland
Coaches	Chicago - Oakland
Reclining Chair Car	Chicago - Oakland
Coach	Pueblo - Oakland (Royal Gorge Route)
Tourist Sleepers	Chicago - Oakland
	Pueblo - Oakland (Royal Gorge Route)
First Class Sleepers	Chicago - Oakland
	Pueblo - Oakland (Royal Gorge Route)
	St. Louis - Oakland (Via Lincoln, Nebraska)
Dining and Observation Cars	Chicago - Oakland

The St. Louis - Oakland sleeping car operated on the General Pershing Zephyr between Lincoln and St. Louis. One might say that such Zephyr service was a prelude to the California Zephyr service introduced in 1949.

The Exposition also offered various other on-board train services. For example, the dining car service was supplemented by economy meals served on trays to passengers at their seats. Porter service was also provided for both coach and chair car passengers as well as pillows. (13)

The Exposition Flyer was powered by the most modern steam locomotives on all three of the railroads. That meant ex-Florida East Coast Railway "Mountain" type 4-8-2s purchased in 1936 by the Western Pacific. The locomotives, originally built by Alco in 1924 were designated Road Class 171, Symbol MTP-44 by the WP. The big 4-8-2s had a tonnage rating virtually twice that of the Ten-wheelers previously assigned to most passenger trains, and were of course, able to operate at higher speeds.

Meanwhile, the Flyer's popularity boosted passenger patronage nearly 7,000 in 1940, and another 11,000 in 1941.

The Feather River Express continued to operate during this time with almost no real attention. She performed the mail and express work and carried a coach and a tourist sleeper on an easy - make all stops - overnight run between Oakland and Portola. The service was scheduled for 11 hours, 40 minutes in both directions, however 30 minutes of this time was part of the ferry service between Oakland Pier and the San Francisco Ferry Building. (14)

The year 1939 brought some minor changes to the WP equipment roster. The company discontinued its lease with General American Tank Car Company for the 25 express refers. Also in that year, the four coach-diners were sold as they had not operated regularly in train service for several years by that time.

The increase enthusiasm on the WP and the other participating railroads brought about the decision to operate the Flyer on a year around basis. An announcement was made on August 27, 1939 that the train would continue operating because of the public's response to the train. (15) The train was really giving the Chicago and North Western, Union Pacific, and Southern Pacific "Overland Route" trains a run for their money. Despite such happiness over the train's patronage and operation, there were dark clouds ahead. Hitler had already invaded Eastern Europe, and American thoughts were tempered with what might lay around the corner. In December, 1941, America found itself in World War II on two fronts and the Nation's Railroads, the Western Pacific included, had to take on new, different, and heavier traffic than ever before. The Western Pacific was to play a major role in troop and military personnel movements to and from the Pacific Front.

Passenger revenues increased by more than 610% between 1939 and 1943. The number of passengers in 1943 hit 509,774, and that was not the peak year. That came in

The Western Pacific operated an extensive list of passenger specials, or "Passenger Extras" to the dispatcher. The next set of photos illustrate a small sample of these trains with the drama and appeal of the Western Pacific.

This photo is unique for several reasons. The train is powered by a 2-8-0, yes a 2-8-0, No. 62; and is a National Railway Historical Society rail-fan excursion train. The photo was taken on June 5, 1938 in Reno, Nevada. Rail fan specials are not new. (Bob Larson Collection)

1945 when 766,925 passengers were carried. The WP had to make many changes.

The Exposition Flyer continued to operate, sometimes with as many as 8 sections during the war. This meant a number of schedule changes had to be made in train operations. For example, prior to 1942, a large percentage of WP passengers were traveling for pleasure. Therefore, the Flyer was operated through the Feather River Canyon in daylight arriving at Oakland in the evening, or departing Oakland in the morning. A study in 1943 revealed that most of the passengers were either military and/or business men with the vacationer being a very small percentage. The schedule was

changed so that the westbound train arrived in Oakland in the morning. The scenic beauties of the Canyon were forgotten for the duration of the war. (16)

The heavy troop movements, naturally, placed a great strain on the average peace time passenger traffic departments. The WP created a military travel bureau within the passenger department to handle this traffic. Also, former on line freight traffic solicitors were then assigned to riding the troop trains to take care of problems that might arise.

The Exposition Flyer also handled additional cars of troops on a daily basis. Most of the regular passengers consisted of officers and soldiers traveling under special orders or on

Some rail fan specials have often consisted of equipment that hardly classified it as a passenger train. This 1954 trip consisted of four mill type gondolas fitted with benches, one standard coach and finally last but not least, a wooden combination car. The 94 itself has been repainted and modified to its early appearance, but still included the classic and traditional Western Pacific insignia on the tender. (Harold K. Vollrath Collection)

furloughs. In addition to the special troop trains, the WP also operated a substantial number of trains carrying laborers en route to the Pacific Coast war production centers and plants. (17)

The Western Pacific handled the war time passenger traffic with a great deal of efficiency, or shall we say with as much as was possible with the tremendous over load that the railroad was under. There were many problems to be sure, but the WP was able to handle them. By 1946, the load was easing, and the total number of passengers was 508,378. In contrast, 1947 saw only 185,657. The Big War was over, and except for the Korean War, passenger patronage would never top 200,000 again. Western Pacific passenger services were literally the opposite of what they were in 1941-42.

train - that of a DOMELINER.   The Flyer made its last trip in March, 1949.

The schedules of trains 1 and 2 were changed to compliment the changes in the Flyer's schedule. However, when the California Zephyr went into operation on March 20, 1949, the name Feather River Express was dropped. Furthermore, trains 1 and 2 became Oakland - Salt Lake City schedules with a new name, The Royal Gorge. Again this secondary schedule was designed to compliment the schedule of the CZ. No. 2 departed Oakland at 6:30 p.m. and arrived at Salt Lake City about 7:45 p.m. The westbound No. 1 departed Salt Lake at 8:30 a.m. with an arrival at Oakland at 7:35 a.m. Equipment included a diner lounge car, coaches and two sleepers: St. Louis and Oakland (8 Sections, 5 Double

Not all special trains handled "Rail-Fans." This May, 1959 edition is a Northwest Life Insurance Company Special. The train consists of 11 cars, and can be classified as an "All-Pullman" special sleeping car train. The special, consisting of two sections, was photographed from the old ice dock in Portola. (Bob Larson)

Meanwhile, new planning was underway.

The success of the Flyer prompted the Burlington, Rio Grande and the WP to consider modernizing and speeding up the service. An order was placed with the Budd Company for the new California Zephyr. However, it would not be until the spring of 1948 before any changes took place. The Flyer was still the only train east of Portola. Trains 1 and 2, however, would also get in on the planning stage.

The Budd Company began delivering the dome coaches during the spring of 1948. At the same time, the three railroads announced that the westbound schedule of the Flyer would be shortened 12 hours permitting daylight travel in the Rockies and the Feather River Canyon effective May 30, 1948. (18) The three companies also planned to operate the dome coaches on the Flyer as soon as they were delivered. And that is exactly what did happen! At the very end of the Flyer's career, it achieved the highest status of a passenger

Bedrooms) and Kansas City - Oakland (Sections, Compartments and Drawing Room, either 8-2-1 or 10-2-1). The train was an excellent secondary run, but the CZ was stealing the entire show, and the Royal Gorge failed to achieve any sizeable patronage.

In 1948 prior to the Zephyr, the WP's passenger count was 160,727, while the next year 1949, it shot up to 195,070.

During the eight months of the Royal Gorge's operation, it carried an average daily load of 60 passengers or approximately 15,000 passengers. The California Zephyr was responsible for an increase of 20,000 passengers all alone in 1949. Furthermore, because of the Royal Gorge's low passenger count, it failed to meet its costs of operation by a net loss of $2,700 per day. In per mile terms, the train grossed $1.19. Expenses equaled $2.69 with the net loss being $1.50 per mile. In December, 1949, President F. B. Whitman wrote in the WP employee magazine, "Mileposts" that efforts were

The Northwest Life Insurance Company Special was a really a big one. While three units were assigned to the section with 11 cars, four units were assigned to the 18 car section, which also included a Southern Pacific baggage car with a wide range of other passenger equipment. (Bob Larson, May, 1959, Portola)

made to increase patronage by leasing modern coaches and by introducing lower coach fares on the train. He added that the company attempted to obtain additional mail revenues and explored the possibilities of obtaining through carload merchandise express business. Also the possibility of handling through cars of less-than-carload freight between the Bay area and Salt Lake City was studied. The company also thought of making 1 and 2 another fast passenger train. But he pointed out that all of the efforts were unsuccessful or the potential of traffic which could be reasonably anticipated failed to approach a level consistent with sound business practice. Mr. Whitman concluded his statements by thanking all of the men involved with the operation and the selling of the Royal Gorge's services for their fine work and spirit, and apologized for having to discontinue the train as such. (19)

However, because of the fact that the WP served some areas that were without all weather roads, some sort of local service had to be continued. It was obvious to the ICC and others that the railroad could not be expected to continue to run the Royal Gorge in its original form. First of all, the sleeping cars and the dining car services were discontinued by the end of 1949. At the same time, the WP cast an eye on the new Rail Diesel Car developed by the Budd Company.

The WP arranged to secure the Budd Company's RDC-1 (full coach)

demonstrator in 1950. The railroad announced in early January that a ten day trial operation would take place with the Budd car on the 600 mile run between Portola and Salt Lake City. Passengers west of Portola continued to ride the steam powered standard train during the January 18th through 27th experimental period. (20)

The reader will recall that trains 1 and 2 operated on a daily basis. The single RDC car could not have handled the daily run for the entire distance. Therefore in order to keep the daily service in effect, and also because express shipments were lighter east of Portola, the run was split at the Eastern - Western Division boundary line. The RDC car ran entirely on the Eastern Division.

For the study, the forward part of the car was stripped of seats and used for head-end traffic which was loaded through the vestibule doors. For the duration of the tests, the Railway Express Agency cooperated by diverting oversize and livestock shipments to either the Southern Pacific or truck.

Obviously all rail-fan specials were not powered by steam either. This 1955, eight car Domeliner "rail-fan" special includes one dome car, a standard lounge observation car (coupled behind the third unit), and what appears to be six standard coaches. The eight car train will be easy work for the three units shown here at San Leandro, California. (Bob Larson)

The Western Pacific placed an order for two RDC-2s, a combination coach and baggage car as a result of the test runs.

During the test, the RDC served as a complete train and proved to be an adequate substitute for the steam powered two car consist of trains 1 and 2. Operational costs were about 50% of the steam train. In 6,000 miles of service, the car averaged 2.8 miles per gallon of fuel at a cost of slightly more than 3 cents per mile. In contrast, the steam operation averaged 22 cents per mile. The terrain over which the tests were conducted included a crossing of Sierra Nevadas at Beckwork Pass, the Nevada Desert with its great winds and the descent from the plateau to the floor of the Great Salt Lake desert where the Bonneville Flats are crossed on a 43 mile tangent. (21) The new RDC-2s were named the Zephyrette and provided tri-weekly service between Oakland and Salt Lake City. More about the Zephyrette in Chapter 5.

With all trains now completely streamlined, the company continued to maintain additional equipment for special trains. There were many such trains operated by the WP over the years. Some of the more famous of these include the 1957 Caribou Country Special. This special operated up the Inside Gateway to the Great Northern, and on up to British Columbia and a connection with the former Pacific Great Eastern (Now the British Columbia Railway). The all expense one week tour carried 185 people at a fare of $250 each.

Still another example was the 1962 Exposition Flyer, an ALL-PULLMAN special which departed the Bay Area for the Seattle World's Fair. The June 30th trip, which was sponsored by the Bay Area Electric Railroad Association, covered seven states, four mountain ranges (Sierras, Rockies, Bitter Roots and the Cascades) plus tours at Salt Lake City, Butte and Yellowstone National Park as well as a two day stop over in Seattle for the Fair.

Other specials were operated for insurance companies, rail fans, company business, and a whole host of other reasons. One of the last passenger specials was powered by Western Pacific GP40, No. 3523, painted in the UP colors with Western Pacific lettering.

As far as standard equipment is concerned, the WP retired its own coaches and baggage cars in 1961. From that time on, the company usually borrowed equipment from the Southern Pacific or other lines for extra or special train service. The last Pullman heavy weight sleepers were taken out of the Pullman lease in 1962, and retired in 1963. Two of the diners remained on the roster until 1968.

The last observation car remained in extra service through 1966.

Two business cars were retired in 1961, but the WP maintained the No. 101 right through the 1970s. Although the Western Pacific passenger car fleet was not as large as most other railroads, it was actually in many ways, more widely known. This was and is especially true with the California Zephyr, the subject of Chapter 4.

(Right) Still another standard passenger trains to operate over the WP was this passenger extra en route from Oakland to Stockton on April 17, 1966. The train, powered by two F-7 diesel units, consisted of eight leased Southern Pacific coaches, a single standard Pullman car painted in the streamlined two tone grey scheme, and the WP's observation lounge. The lounge car operated backwards behind the power on this east bound run which is shown here passing San Leandro, at mile post 14.8 miles east of San Francisco. (Author's Collection)

Company business also required special passenger trains. In this case, we have a clearance train, that is, special equipment designed to measure the clearances in tunnels, snow sheds, and bridges. Two units are assigned to the three car train: a clearance measuring car, a laboratory rider coach, and finally a business car. With the two F units, and the standard passenger equipment, the train definitely falls into the "classic" status. These types of trains are also fun to model. (Bob Larson)

Source Note:

All figures of passenger patronage and passenger miles were drawn from Poor's Railroad Volumes 1913 to 1940, and from Moody's Transportation Volumes 1941 to 1970.

Endnotes:

1 and 2. Western Pacific Historical Notes.
3 to 11 are from RAILWAY AGE as per dates listed below:
3. May 31, 1931, p. 1049.
4. March 17, 1934, p. 375.
5. June 2, 1934, p. 824.
6. Ibid.
7. June 18, 1938, p. 1028.
8. February 25, 1939, p. 353.
9. March 25, 1939, p. 536.
10. June 17, 1939, p. 1052.
11. Ibid.
12 and 14. Western Pacific Railroad Passenger Time Table, July 20, 1939.
13 and 15.. RAILWAY AGE, September 2, 1939, p. 353.
16 through 18, and 20 and 21 from RAILWAY AGE:
16 and 17. 1943, page 614.
18. March 27, 1948, p. 639.
20. January 14, 1950, p. 44.
21. March 4, 1950, p. 67
19. "The Royal Gorge Passenger Train," MILEPOSTS, San Francisco, California: Western Pacific Railroad Company, December, 1949.

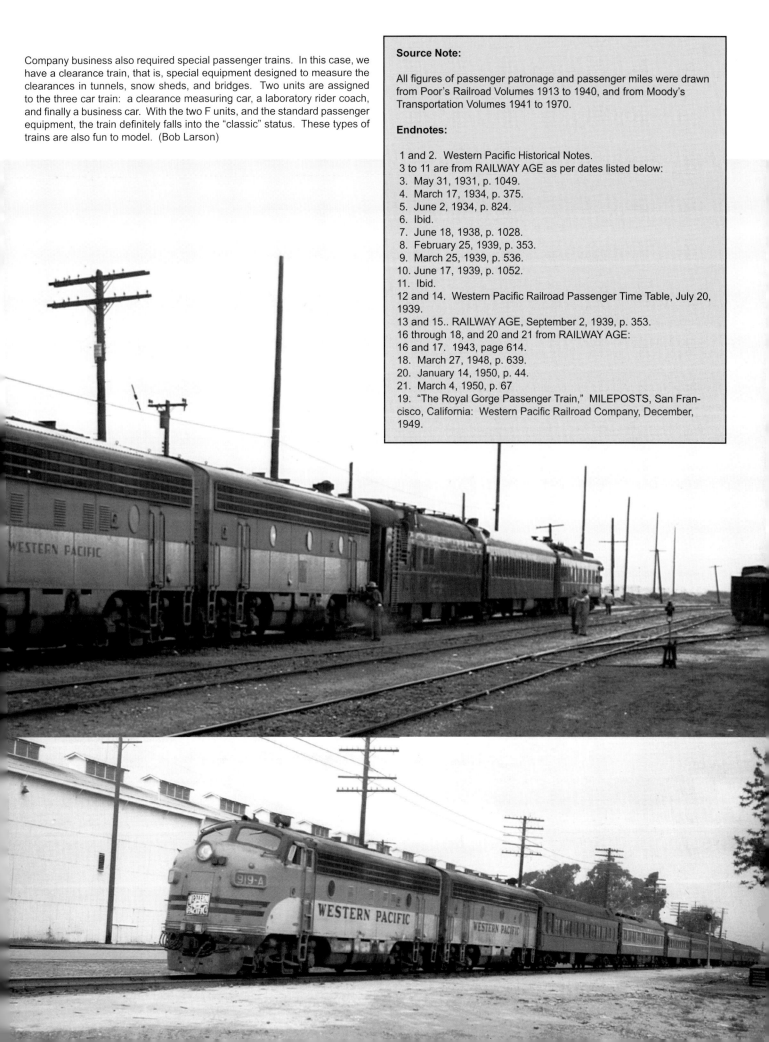

It is October 8, 1971, and WP's Business Car No. 1 is part of the consist of a Union Pacific freight train at Valley, Nebraska. The car is running backwards just ahead of the UP caboose at the end of the train. (Lou Schmitz)

Western Pacific passenger train services could be handled on literally one page, including branch lines and connections during the Great Depression. (Western Pacific Railroad, Local Time Folder, May 15, 1935)

READ DOWN 2 Daily "Scenic Limited"	Miles	Pacific Time MAIN LINE	Elevation	READ UP 1 Daily "Scenic Limited"
7 00	0	Lv....San Francisco....Ar		8 50
7 28	4	Lv....Oakland Pier....Ar	14	8 20
7 40	7	Lv.Oakland (3rd & Wash.).Ar	18	8 10
7 50	10	Lv.Oakland (Fruitvale)..Lv	34	f 7 56
f 8 02	15	Lv....San Leandro....Lv	48	f 7 44
f 8 10	20	Lv....Hayward....Lv	99	f 7 36
8 25	30	Lv....Niles....Lv	68	7 23
	36	Lv....Sunol....Lv	254	f 6 58
f 8 45	41	Lv....Pleasanton....Lv	341	f 7 04
f 8 55	48	Lv....Livermore....Lv	480	f 6 55
	57	Lv....Altamont....Lv	752	
	72	Lv....Carbona....Lv	135	
	74	Lv....Lyoth....Lv	80	
	84	Lv....Lathrop....Lv	22	
10 05	94	Lv....Stockton....Lv	23	5 40
	105	Lv....Kingdon....Lv	27	
f 10 36	114	Lv....Thornton....Lv	20	f 5 05
	119	Lv....Glannvale....Lv	22	
f 10 53	125	Lv....Franklin....Lv	25	f 4 46
	129	Lv....Runyon....Lv	29	
	136	Lv...South Sacramento...Lv	28	
11 25	139	Ar....Sacramento....Lv	23	4 25
		Connection Sacto. Nor. Ry.		
f 11 53	156	Lv....Pleasant Grove....Lv	48	
f 12 01	162	Lv....Trowbridge....Lv	57	
	173	Lv....Arboga....Lv	66	
12 30	179	Lv....Marysville....Lv	86	3 20
		Connection Sacto. Nor. Ry.		
	193	Lv....Craig....Lv	103	
	199	Lv....Palermo....Lv	165	
1 10	205	Ar....Oroville....Lv	203	2 45
1 20	205	Lv....Oroville....Ar	203	2 35
		Sacramento Northern Ry.		
	213	Lv....Bidwell....Lv	332	f 2 17
	218	Lv....Bloomer....Lv	418	f 2 29
f..	221	Lv....Las Plumas....Lv	562	f..
	224	Lv....Berry Creek....Lv	693	
	229	Lv....Blinzig....Lv	897	f 3 56
	231	Lv....Isaiah....Lv	988	f..
2 35	239	Lv....Pulga....Lv	1380	1 25
	241	Lv....Mayaro....Lv	1452	f..
f 2 48	244	Lv....Cresta....Lv	1580	f 1 11
	248	Lv....Merlin....Lv	1758	f..
	249	Lv....Rock Creek....Lv	1836	f..
	251	Lv....Storrie....Lv	1897	f..
3 13	253	Lv....Tobin....Lv	2006	f 12 48
f 3 20	256	Lv....Camp Rodgers....Lv	2128	f 12 42
3 33	260	Lv....Belden....Lv	2382	12 32
	262	Lv....Howells....Lv	2382	f..
f 3 45	265	Lv....Rich....Lv	2502	f 12 18
f 3 59	270	Lv....Virgilia....Lv	2752	f 12 05
f..	273	Lv....Gray's Flat....Lv	2900	f..
4 09	274	Lv....Twain....Lv	2909	11 56
4 19	278	Lv....Paxton....Lv	3080	11 47
		Connection Indian Valley R. R.		
4 32	281	Lv....Keddie....Lv	3227	11 38
	285	Lv....Sierra (Oakland Municipal Camp)..Lv	3438	
4 52	288	Ar....Quincy Jct....Lv	3545	11 21
		Connection Quincy Railroad		
	292	Lv....Massack....Lv	3759	f 11 09
5 13	297	Lv.Spg. Garden..Williams Loop	3964	f 10 50
f 5 26	302	Lv....Sloat....Lv	4117	f 10 50
	303	Lv....Cromberg....Lv	4179	
	306	Lv....Two Rivers....Lv	4260	
f 5 45	309	Lv..Feather River Inn..Lv	4374	f 10 36
5 52	310	Lv....Blairsden....Lv	4414	10 34
f 6 02	314	Lv....Clio....Lv	4577	f 10 25
6 20	321	Ar....Portola....Lv	4834	10 10

READ DOWN 2 Daily "Scenic Limited"	Miles	Pacific Time MAIN LINE	Elevation	READ UP 1 Daily "Scenic Limited"
6 30	321	Lv....Portola....Ar	4834	10 00
	326	Lv....Calpine Junction....Lv	4874	
		Connection Calpine Branch		
	327	Lv....Beckwourth....Lv	4874	
	328	Lv....Hawley....Lv	4875	
		Connection Loyalton Branch		
	332	Lv....Hindoo....Lv	4889	
	340	Lv....Chilcoot....Lv	5003	f 9 32
	342	Lv....Reno Junction....Lv	4986	f 9 27
		Connection Reno Branch		
	346	Lv....Scotts....Lv	4817	
	358	Lv....Omira....Lv	4353	
7 37	363	Lv....Doyle....Lv	4262	8 48
	372	Lv....Hackstaff....Lv	4119	
	378	Lv....Calneva, Cal....Lv	4008	
	384	Lv....Flanigan, Nev....Lv	3998	
	394	Lv....Sand Pass....Lv	4199	
	424	Lv....Bronte....Lv	3856	
9 35	438	Lv....Gerlach....Lv	3931	6 52
	471	Lv....Ronda....Lv	4044	
f 10 26	475	Lv....Sulphur....Lv	4042	f 5 56
f 11 03	497	Lv....Jungo....Lv	4167	f 5 20
	515	Lv....Pronto....Lv	4238	
12 05	532	Lv....Winnemucca....Lv	4334	4 30
	536	Lv....Weso....Weso	4305	
f 12 28	549	Lv....Golconda....Golconda	4346	f 4 01
f 12 44	562	Lv.Red House..Comus..Lv	4380	
	575	Lv....Ellison..Valmy....Lv	4380	
f 1 16	589	Lv.N.Battle Mt..Battle Mt..Lv	4501	f 3 14
	601	Lv....Kampos..Argenta..Lv	4550	
	610	Lv....Dunphy..Shoshone..Lv	4631	
f 1 55	619	Lv....Beowawe..Beowawe..Lv	4696	f 2 39
	627	Lv....Cluro..Cluro....Lv	4737	
f 2 17	635	Lv....Palisade..Palisade..Lv	4844	f 2 14
2 29	645	Lv....Carlin..Carlin..Lv	4809	1 58
3 10	665	Lv....Elko..Elko....Lv	5061	1 23
	683	Lv....Elburz..Elburz..Lv	5206	
	688	Lv....Halleck..Halleck..Lv	5230	
f 3 56	699	Lv....Deeth..Deeth..Lv	5341	f 12 35
	709	Lv....Tulasco..Tulasco..Lv	5510	
f 4 20	714	Lv....Alazon..Alazon..Lv	5502	f 12 13
	717	Lv....Wells..Lv	5631	
f 4 43	728	Lv....Ruby..Lv	5771	f 11 51
	733	Lv....Tobar..Lv	5685	
	739	Lv....Ventosa..Lv	5602	f 11 24
	753	Lv....Jasper..Lv	5868	
	757	Lv....Luke..Lv	5590	
5 36	766	Lv....Shafter..Lv	5594	11 01
		Connection Nevada Northern		
	772	Lv....Silver Zone....Lv	5821	
	774	Lv....Arnold..Arnolds Lv	5827	
	783	Lv....Proctor..Loop Lv	5392	
	789	Lv....Pilot..Lv	5138	
	799	Lv....Ola, Nevada..Lv	4608	
6 40	806	Ar..Wendover, Utah..Lv	4246	9 35
6 45	806	Lv..Wendover, Utah..Lv	4246	9 25
		Connection Deep Creek R. R.		
	815	Lv....Salduro....Lv	4222	
	825	Lv....Arinosa..Salt Lv	4223	
	835	Lv....Barro..Beds Lv	4226	
	845	Lv....Knolls..Lv	4230	
f 8 17	878	Lv....Delle..Lv	4270	f 7 56
	886	Lv....Timpie..Lv	4226	
	893	Lv....Ellerbeck..Lv	4222	
f 8 41	897	Lv....Burmester..Lv	4224	f 7 28
	902	Lv....Spray..Great Lv	4215	
	908	Lv....Lago..Salt Lv	4215	
	913	Lv....Garfield..Lake Lv	4232	
	921	Lv....Fox..Lv	4237	
9 30	928	Ar..Salt Lake City, Utah..Lv	4233	6 45
		(Pacific Time)		
10 30	928	Ar..Salt Lake City, Utah..Lv	4233	7 45
		(Mountain Time)		

BRANCH LINES

READ DOWN 314 Mixed	Mls.	Calpine Branch	READ UP 313 Mixed
e 8 00	0	Lv....Portola....Ar	5 00
8 30	5	Lv....Calpine Jct....Lv	11 30
9 30	17	Ar....Calpine....Lv	c10 30

READ DOWN 416 Mixed	Mls.	Loyalton Branch	READ UP 415 Mixed
e 8 00	0	Lv....Portola....Ar	5 00
12 01	7	Lv....Hawley....Lv	3 30
1 01	19	Ar....Loyalton....Lv	c 2 30

READ DOWN 220 Mixed	Mls.	Reno Branch	READ UP 219 Mixed
* 1 30	0	Lv....Portola....Ar	12 20
2 45	20	Lv....Reno Jct....Ar	11 26
f 2 57	23	Lv....Plumas....Lv	11 07
f 3 18	30	Lv....Feavine....Lv	f10 44
f 3 37	36	Lv....Copperfield....Lv	f10 27
f 3 45	38	Lv....Anderson....Lv	f10 20
4 30	53	Ar....Reno....Lv	* 9 30

CONNECTIONS

INDIAN VALLEY RAILROAD

2	Mls.	STATIONS	1
‡8 00	0	Lv....Paxton....Ar	1 00
8 15	4	Ar....Indian Falls....Ar	12 45
8 30	8	Ar....Crescent Mills....Lv	‡12 30

QUINCY RAILROAD

2	Mls.	STATIONS	1
*11 21	4 52	Lv..Quincy Jct....Ar	4 40	11 10
11 45	5 20	Ar....Quincy....Lv	*4 10	*10 50

EUREKA NEVADA RAILWAY

1	Mls.	STATIONS	2
‡ 8 15	0	Lv....Palisade....Ar	2 00
3 00	85	Ar....Eureka....Lv	b 7 15

NEVADA CENTRAL RAILROAD

53	Mls.	STATIONS	54
‡ 9 20	0	Lv..Battle Mountain..Lv	1 40
3 00	93	Ar....Austin....Lv	‡ 8 15

NEVADA NORTHERN RAILWAY

4	Mls.	STATIONS	3
* 3 31	0	Lv....Shafter....Ar	11 59
6 46	113	Ar....McGill....Lv	8 35
7 25	121	Lv....East Ely....Lv	8 05
7 30	122	Ar....Ely....Lv	* 8 00

DEEP CREEK RAILROAD

MASON MOORE, MGR., WENDOVER, UTAH

81	Mls.	STATIONS	82
k 9 45	0	Lv....Wendover....Ar	6 00
f12 01	37	Ar..Garrison Monster..Lv	f 3 35
12 45	45	Ar....Gold Hill....Lv	k 2 45

Reference Marks:

‖Meals. fFlag Stop. *Daily. ‡Daily except Sunday. b—Daily except Monday.

c—Tuesdays, Thursdays and Saturdays only. e—Tuesdays only. k—Fridays only.

Time from 12:01 midnight to 12:00 noon is shown by LIGHT faced figures, and time from 12:01 noon to 12:00 midnight by HEAVY faced figures.

NOTICE:—This Company will not be responsible for errors in time tables, inconvenience or damage resulting from delayed trains or failure to make connections; schedules herein are subject to change without notice.

TELEGRAPH SERVICE

For the convenience of our passengers Western Union Telegraph service is available from many stations. If you wish, you may hand your message to the train conductor or porter who will see that it is transmitted from the next station at which train stops.

EXPRESS YOUR PACKAGES

Convenient and fast express service for your packages is available at every Express Agency along the lines of this Railroad.

File A. D.-14—5-6-35—55M

This Western Division photo of the California Zephyr says it all. It delivers the message the WP wanted to portray about itself and the Zephyr when this publicity photo was taken in the CZ's career. Mountains, forest lands, domes, a safe-and-secure trip - all to be synonymous with the Western Pacific, which is proudly displayed across the nose of F-3 No. 801.

Only part of the consist of the domeliner is visible in the photo, which in itself was designed to wet the appetite of the prospective train rider. "Look at those dome cars. What else is on this train?" This photo was also taken for part of the co-operative advertising, marketing and public relations program for all three railroads operating the CZ. (Western Pacific Photo, Author's Collection)

Chapter 4

THE CALIFORNIA ZEPHYR

Sometimes known as the "Most Talked About Train in the Country," the California Zephyr is also probably one of the most written about trains in the country too. Who can deny that the CZ was not a great train? If the CZ were literally duplicated today in 2006, perhaps with head-end power instead of steam heating, etc. and a few other technological changes for safety and comfort; but with the exterior and interior decor matching the 1949 train, it would still be considered a very modern passenger train. The train was simply just that good! In fact, the CZ was so good and had such a drawing power that people would fly from New York to Chicago and take the CZ west.

The California Zephyr was conceived during a period of time when streamliners were the rage throughout North America. Jet airliners were being studied by the British,

but domestic airlines had given only lip service to the idea. As mentioned in the previous chapter, the Burlington, Rio Grande and the Western Pacific finalized the plans for this "Domeliner" in 1947. The Budd Company was given the job of constructing the 69 cars that would be used to assemble 6 eleven car sets for the daily Chicago - Oakland service. In the original order, there were three extra 10 roomette, 6 double bedroom sleeping cars. One of these, the Silver Rapids, was owned by the Pennsylvania Railroad for transcontinental New York - San Francisco service. The Rio Grande also ordered an additional 16 section Sleeper. (1) Six 6 Double Bedroom, 5 Compartment sleepers were placed in service in 1952, and at the same time, the CB&Q purchased an additional observation car. Altogether 77 CZ cars were built with 26 of the fleet owned by the Western Pacific.

When the California Zephyr was placed in service in 1949, and throughout most of the 1950s, trains 17 and 18 were basically an eleven car train throughout the entire year. However, during the summers and Christmas - New Year's Holiday Seasons, the train frequently carried an additional coach and one or two extra sleeping cars. The typical consist prior to 1952 was as follows: (2, 3)

```
1 Baggage Car
3 Dome Coaches (Designated CZ 20, 21 and 22)
1 Dome Buffet Lounge Dormitory Car
1 Dining Car
2 Ten Roomette, Six Double Bedroom cars (CZ14 and 15)
1 Sixteen Section Sleeping Car (CZ12)
1 Ten Roomette, Six Double Bedroom car (CZ11 to and
from New York City)
1 Three Bedroom, Drawing Room Dome observation
Lounge Car (CZ10)
```

The three railroads designated the Six Double Bedroom, Five Compartment cars as CZ16 when they were placed in service in 1952.

The 16 Section cars continued to operate, first on a year around basis, and then on a seasonal basis through 1962. At that time, the regular running of the car was discontinued and the WP converted its 16 Section cars to 48 seat coaches, the only flat top streamlined coaches the company ever owned. From 1962 on, only room sleeping cars operated on a regular basis on the California Zephyr.

The summer time tables also listed the flat top coach as part of the regular train consist, usually designated CZ23. Summer consists were often 13 cars or more reducing to the standard 11 during the rest of the year. However, from 1967 on, the WP's consist during the off season was often only nine or ten cars with one less dome coach, and/or one less 10-6 sleeping car. The train continued to run with a full complement of lounge and dining car services right until the end of WP participation in the train's operation in March, 1970.

As mentioned before, the CZ was a master piece of construction by the Budd Company. There were two types of dome coaches operated in each train. Both types provided seating for 46 passengers plus 24 in the dome. The six seats next to the bulkheads adjacent to the domes (seat numbers 25 through 30) did not include

leg rests nor did they recline. Whenever possible, these seats were assigned to short distance or local passengers. Lighting was provided by cylindrical magnifying ceiling units. As one would go up stairs to the dome, lighting gradually changed from high to low density so that reflections on the dome glass windows would not restrict the passengers' ability to see out. (2)

Originally the passageway of the first coach in each train contained a swinging door which divided the forward section from the rest of the car. During the early career of the CZ, this section was reserved for women and children only. The women's room in all of the coaches were fitted with electrical receptacles for a bottle warmer which could be obtained from the hostess.

The second dome coach in each was slightly different from the other two cars by using a 3 foot, 6 inch space in the vestibule end of the car for a conductor's booth. This space, which was used as a baggage space in the other two cars, was fitted with a seat, desk and locker. Across the aisle from the little office were the regulator and control lockers.

There were three color schemes for the dome coaches. The first one used a Burgundy carpet, wood tone upholstery in the coach sections, and Mahogany in the dome. These colors were combined with light Indian Red on the wainscot and orchid gray on the sides and ceiling. The Venetian blinds matched the walls but were relieved with Indian Red tapes.

The second car combined a green carpet and turquoise upholstery with coconut brown wainscot, coconut beige sides and a cafe au lait ceiling. The third car had a brown carpet, rush upholstery, walls of two tone nut pine, and light dust tone on the ceiling. Venetian blinds matched the walls and had dark tapes.

Directly behind the coaches was the Vista Dome Buffet Lounge Dormitory car. This car included the famous "Cable Car Room" and served light meals and beverages from the early morning until the late evening. The car was decorated

One of the namesakes for the Western Pacific was the Feather River Canyon. This view shows the CZ in the Canyon with all of its glory, magnitude and everlasting beauty. (TLC Publishing Collection)

The train was not only popular with the traveling public for many years, but it was also popular with railroad enthusiasts. Rail Photo Service once had a complete catalogue of CZ photos on all railroads. In this photo, the CZ, No. 17, is pausing at Fremont, California on the first Subdivision of the former Western Division. (Photo by B. F. Cutler, Rail Photo Service, Author's Collection)

in beige and tan colors. The "Cable Car Room," located forward of the dome, contained a large mural at one end of the room. This mural made it appear as though the room itself were a cable car going up a San Francisco street. There was also a conductor's signal cord dangling from the ceiling just before the mural for a realistic effect. There were also models of cable cars attached to the walls of the unique room. The seats were decorated in red. The lounge beneath the dome was also beige in color with black seats and pictures of cable cars on the walls. There was also a bar with a large service window. Immediately beyond the bar was a buffet kitchen from which sandwiches, coffee, and other beverages were served. The equipment included a combination coffee and hot water urn, toaster, ice cream box, sinks and a dish washer.

The steward and the hostess each had a bedroom in the dormitory section of this car. Forward of these bedrooms

was the dorm section with five sets of three tier bunks. There was also a toilet, washroom, and shower facilities for the crew.

The next car in the train was the dining car. The focal point was the steward's desk and its back mirror. The front of the desk was a carved and painted linoleum scene. The carpet was green in a geometrical pattern. The upholstery was leather. It was green with yellow piping on the seats at the ends of the room, and rose on the chairs in the main section of the room. The wainscot was gray green with an ecru ceiling and sides. The drapes had bright colored figures on an ivory background. Each table in the dining room received fresh carnations daily.

The kitchen and the pantry was stainless steel. Electrical facilities included a dish washer, glass washer, juicer, refrigerators, a large range, sinks and two exhaust fans.

Advance dinner reservations were required which elimi-

Ultimately, FP7s were purchased by the WP and assigned to the California Zephyr, such as the 804D and two "B" units on the head-end at Oakland, California on July 30, 1958. (T.W. Dixon Collection)

There is no doubt about it! The dome was and is the greatest travel innovation ever invented. To simply say, "Look up, down and all around," just doesn't give the real travel thrill until one actually experiences it.

This writer heard a joke several years ago that two women were riding in a dome car and watching the block signals turn red after the head-end of the train went past the signal. One said to the other, "The engineer is barely making the green lights." (Western Pacific Photo, Author's Collection)

nated waiting in line for a table. The menu features a choice of traditional favorites as well as regional delicacies cooked to the passenger's order. Several dishes throughout the years on the CZ had an Italian flavor because that type of cooking was once featured. Examples of dinner included Antipasti, Chicken Cacciatore, Ravioli, Spaghetti and Veal Scaloppini A La Parmesan. The seating capacity of the dining room ranged from 40 to 48 passengers depending upon the number of two seat tables in the car. (4)

During the 21 years of operation, there were three types of Pullman sleeping cars in regular service on trains 17 and 18, The most prevalent were the 10-6 type cars. However, the exteriors of the equipment did not show the word "Pullman" anywhere. The letter board proudly displayed the name "California Zephyr." It was one of the last three major trains in the United States to carry its name in the "Letter Boards." (The other two being the Empire Builder and the City of Miami.) The sublettering on the corners of the cars denoted railroad ownership.

For most of the CZ's career three 10-6 sleepers were operated in the consist. At the time of their construction, these sleeping cars were of the most advanced sleeping car design. At the end of each car, near the vestibule in a longitudinal space of about six feet was a toilet room, the electrical regulator, and the control lockers on one side. Across the aisle was the porter's area which included a locker, a seat, a bedding locker, and high folding berth which was screened from the aisle by a curtain when made up.

Ten roomettes, five on each side, adjoined the porter's area. Each roomette contained a mirror opposite the seat,

which contributed to a sense of spaciousness. There was a full length mirror inside the sliding aisle door and a full length wardrobe closet at the side of the seat. There was space for luggage under the seat and in a parcel rack over the mirror. In the rear section of the car were the six double bedrooms. Transverse and longitudinal rooms alternated and folding partition walls permitted them to be joined in pairs to form a suite. In the daytime, each transverse room had a sofa with folding arm rests for three passengers. The lower berth was made up by folding down the back of the sofa and the upper was hinged above the sofa. The lower in the longitudinal room operated in the same manner as the bed in the roomette. (The roomette bed folded down from the wall.) In addition to the seat of the roomette type, there was an upholstered chair which could be folded and stored under the lower bed at night. The upper, which occupied the usual position against the ceiling adjoining the passageway position. To make it up, it was rolled across the ceiling on tracks which caused the leading edge of the berth to drop

This scene shows the roof detail of lead unit No. 801 and the two trailing B units as the CZ approaches Williams Look and is about to pass under the upper level track. (B. F. Cutler, Rail Photo Service, Author's Collection)

FP7A No. 804D is showing signs of needing a paint job, but nevertheless is on the job leading two B units on train 18 loading passengers at the Third Street Depot in Oakland. (July, 1965, Author's Collection)

drawing room and three double bedrooms, two of which were longitudinal and one was transverse. The interior was similar to the other sleeping car rooms in the train.

Besides the five vista domes, the CZ had several features. Each train was staffed with a hostess, called a Zephyrette. The train was scheduled to travel through the Rockies and the Sierra Nevada mountains in daylight. On the WP, the Zephyr crossed the Sierras at Beckworth Pass and then it followed the Feather River for many miles. The scenery and the unspoiled wilderness in Colorado and California were part of the train's greatest selling points.

The trains were also equipped with radio and public address systems. Two "two-spool" wire reproducers gave 12 hours of continuous entertainment. There was also a telephone system by which members of the train crew could communicate between certain points in the train.

The Western Pacific constructed a fully equipped coach servicing yard and diesel locomotive shop to service and maintain the new Zephyr. The make up of the $880,000 Oakland facility included a repair shop, store building, general utility building, a boiler and lathe building, a truck repair

on tracks which caused the leading edge of the berth to drop down gradually to position as it approached the side of the car. The front of the berth was then lowered against a counterweight spring by turning a handle which released it from the track. It was supported at one end on a bracket on the partition and at the other end by a steel rod from the ceiling, which was put in place by the porter.

Each of the rooms, including the roomettes, had a toilet and sink. In the bedrooms, the toilet areas were enclosed and contained a wash basis and toilet. All of the toilet rooms in the train were floored with ceramic tile.

The 16 Section sleeper did not contain room accommodations. This style of car contained men's and women's dressing rooms located at opposite ends of the car.

The 6 Double Bedroom, 5 Compartment sleeping cars were built with the same design styles as the 10-6 sleepers.

The last car of the train was the dome sleeper observation lounge car. This car featured scenic murals, and was carpeted in a brownish rose. The upholstery in the dome was green needlepoint while in the lounge section it was divided between sand and brown. The lower walls were rose tan while the upper walls and ceiling were beige. The drapes were gold and white. The car also contained a three passenger

A close up view of FP7 805A on the head end of No. 18 prior to departure from Oakland on September 1, 1959. (T. W. Dixon Collection)

shop, commissary building, car washing layout, and a five track yard. This facility housed and serviced the CZ during its approximately 19 hour stay every day during its 21 year career. The WP also operated a train washing facility at Portola where the Zephyr was washed every morning before completing the last leg of the journey through the Sierras to Oakland.

It is a cloudy day, but no less thrilling for riding the CZ as No. 17 arrives at Oakland with 11 cars. It is December, 1967 with the Holiday Rush right around the corner. What an incredible way to start the Holiday Season, but with a ride on a train - especially the California Zephyr. (T. W. Dixon Collection)

When the Zephyr passenger cars were constructed, they went through a series of brake tests and shake down runs. On the WP, the train went on display at San Francisco and conducted several exhibition runs from San Francisco to Niles and return on March 16, 17, and 18 in 1949. The WP Christened the CZ with a bottle of California champagne wielded by movie star Eleanor Parker on March 19th. The ceremony took place at the Ferry Building on San Francisco's waterfront. (5)

After the ceremonies, there was a luncheon for business and civic leaders, an address of welcome by Mayor Leland Cutler, a presentation of the train by WP's president H. A. Mitchell, and its acceptance on behalf of the people of California by Lieutenant Governor Goodwin J. Knight. It was a very joyful day to say the least.

The Zephyr made its first eastbound trip on March 20th. Every woman on board that first trip received a corsage of three Hawaiian Orchids in the CZ colors of orange and silver. The train was given a send off by the WP employee's band. Passengers on board included the first 1949 "trade trip" party of the San Francisco Chamber of Commerce en route to Salt Lake City, Utah. The Zephyr had begun its 21 year career.

An interesting side light concerning the train consist took place during the first few months of operation. When the CZ was first placed in service, the dome buffet lounge car - intended primarily for use of the coach passengers - was placed behind the three coaches and two of the bedroom - roomette sleeping cars. The full dining car, two sleepers and the observation car followed. This arrangement tended to draw passengers from the two forward sleeping cars into the buffet car for beverage service. The presence of the passengers enjoying the various refreshments changed the atmosphere of the car to that of a club lounge car, which in turn dissuaded coach passengers from partaking of the a la carte buffet snack service. This placed an additional burden on the dining car, which was being taxed by heavier than anticipated patronage. The consist of the train was then rearranged so that the full diner was between the buffet and all of the sleeping cars. This arrangement continued until the end of CZ service in 1970. This new positioning influenced Pullman passengers to move to the observation lounge for beverage service. Coach patronage of the buffet snack service increased as the refreshment trade shifted to the rear of the train.

The silver and orange color scheme of the Western Pacific motive power was a perfect match for the silver color scheme of the CZ passenger equipment. 804D is doing the honors on this summer day in July, 1958. (T. W. Dixon Collection)

Did the California Zephyr ever run in multiple sections? Yes indeed! Take July 3, 1966 for example. The 805D leads 1st No. 17 at Portola, California, which in this case happens to be a Shriner's Special. (Bob Larson Collection)

On June 1, 1949, cold plate meals were added to the a la carte menu with the idea of making available to passengers an inexpensive meal service, and at the same time further relieve the dining car. The service of the cold plate meals from the small one man buffet kitchen was handled by substitution of paper plate services except for coffee, cereals, and liquor relieving the cook of most of his dishwashing duties.

After the CZ had been in operation for three months, the accountants released figures that showed the "profit" picture. The train was earning $1.29 per train mile, or in other words, the CZ was placing 36.5% of the gross revenue in the net income column. Three years later, the CZ was earning $1.19 per train mile. The three railroads were earning approximately $800,000 per year on their $18 million investment. However, this investment figure did not include such items as the new Oakland coach yard, or the new WP ticket office placed in service in 1953 in Salt Lake City.

Other new innovations came along from time to time. For example, on June 16, 1954, the WP joined the family fare plan. One of the first tickets sold was to a family of 11 children en route to Wisconsin. According to the Western Pacific, the family saved nearly $500 over the previous fares.

The CZ was ten years old in March, 1959. During that period of time, the domeliner carried an average passenger load of 89.4% the year around. The train had also run more than 18,500,000 miles and carried more than 1,500,000 passengers. (6)

About eighteen months later, August 22, 1960 to be exact, the CZ was involved in another WP celebration. On that day, the CZ arrived in Oakland behind ten wheeler No. 94, the same locomotive that brought the first passenger train into Oakland fifty years previously. The Western Pacific brought the locomotive out of retirement to do the honors for the historic event. President F. B. Whitman, who began his railroad career as a locomotive fireman in 1919, was in the cab of No. 94 and took part in the welcoming ceremonies after the CZ arrived in Oakland.

During the celebration it was noted that in the fifty years of WP passenger services, the company had operated 5.5 billion passenger miles of service with but one passenger fatality in a train accident. This fact is not only a tribute to Western Pacific's Safety Record, but also the potential of railroad passenger transportation safety in general.

After 1960, changes took place that adversely affected the CZ. For one thing since 1956, the train's profit and loss statement had gone from black to red ink. The Western Pa-

Second No. 17 with the 804D for powering the regular CZ is a bit late and behind the 1st Section at Portola. (Bob Larson Collection)

cific, being the furthest west of the triple alliance, felt the red ink first since it did not have an overnight market, such as Chicago - Denver, or a Colorado Ski Resort market on its line. The WP tried to stem the loss by adding Flexi-Van cars to 17 and 18 in 1964. That didn't work! A year later, the three roads tried to secure a mail contract for the transcontinental run. That didn't materialize either. The Western Pacific's operating losses increased year after year. In 1964, the loss was $497,300. (7) It jumped to $816,700 in 1965, and was over $500,000 for the first six months of 1966. The situation was very

The Zephyr was only a few weeks old when this portrait of No. 17 was taken a Pleasanton, California on the First Sub-division of the Western Division. No. 801 is leading 17 at the maximum allowable speed going through town, which in those days was 50 miles per hour. (Bob Larson Collection)

bleak for the WP. The ironic thing about the CZ case was that this was not the usual situation of declining patronage. In fact, from 1950 through 1965, the number of passengers was relatively stable. The 1950 figure was 138,588, while in 1965 it was 135,553. It was a case of rising costs without a corresponding rise in railroad fares. It was a real dilemma and the WP felt that the only solution to financial drain was to discontinue the service.

Originally, the WP sought to discontinue the train in September, 1966, but the ICC ordered the train to continue running for at least one year; and it continued the order until 1970. From 1966 through 1969 the proceedings with the ICC were nothing short of a complete nightmare. During this time, not only did expenses continue to sky rocket, over $2 million was lost by the WP in 1969, but revenues also began to slide. REA Express revenue went from $121,500 in 1964 to 0 in 1967. The 1965 passenger load average was 78%. From that time on, it too began to slide. In 1968, for example, the WP's revenue dipped to $1,902,000. It was the first time since 1949 that WP revenues were below $2 million. The California Zephyr had become one of the sadist tales of American Railroading. (8)

It is of significance that during all this time, the WP did not down grade the service. There were various proposals to provide tri-weekly service, reduce equipment consists, and even reduce maintenance. All of these proposals would have simply hastened the all ready sky rocketing costs. It was almost like a case of the city bus line. To cut service, and raise fares only increases losses instead of improving the situation. The WP was wise not to succumb to such tactics. And

as we all know, the California Zephyr - the "Most Talked About Train in the Country" became an item of railroad history in March, 1970. The Western Pacific Railroad became "All - Freight." (9, 10)

Eventually Amtrak renamed the Chicago - Bay Area service the California Zephyr. The train operates over the Burlington Northern Santa Fe between Chicago and Denver, and hence the Union Pacific's Rio Grande lines to Salt Lake City, and partially over the former WP trackage west of Salt Lake City. See Chapter 6 for a brief commentary on Amtrak's Superliner, THE CALIFORNIA ZEPHYR.

Endnotes:

1. "Six Trains for California Zephyr Service," RAILWAY AGE, March 16, 1949, p. 636.
2. "Vista Domes on the Newest Transcontinental Route," RAILWAY AGE, March 26, 1949, p. 646.
3. Western Pacific Time Tables, 1950 issues.
4. "Dining Car Strategy," RAILWAY AGE, August 27, 1949.
5. "Western Pacific Christen California Zephyr," RAILWAY AGE, March 26, 1949, p. 665.
6. "The California Zephyr is 10 Years Old," RAILWAY AGE, March 30, 1959, p. 68.
7. "California Zephyr Gets Another Chance," RAILWAY AGE, October 4, 1965, p. 7.
8. "ICC Orders WP to Keep the Zephyr Going," RAILWAY AGE, January 5-12, 1970, p. 12.
9. "The ICC Relents - CZ Will Come Off," RAILWAY AGE, February 23, 1970, p. 11.
10. "Farewell to the Cal Zephyr," RAILWAY AGE, March 30, 1970, p. 8.

Another example of the superb scenery visible from the California Zephyr. The 804A is leading No. 18 through the west switch at Merlin, California on the Third Subdivision of the Western Division. (Bob Larson, July, 1959)

This photo in many ways dramatizes the safety of railroad operations. In this case, train 17 eases up the main line, while Extra 909A East waits in the hole at James, California on the Third Subdivision of the Western Division. When 17 has cleared the switch, the CTC signal will turn yellow or green for eastbound extra to move out on the main line and continue its trip east. (Bob Larson, August, 1963)

Sometimes difficulties would arise, such as derailments or washouts, and CZ would have to detour over the Southern Pacific. It is September 13, 1964, and such an event has taken place. Therefore, WP GP9, No. 729, is now listed as Passenger Extra 729 East and will pull the westbound CZ backwards to Reno via Reno Junction. At that point, the train will re-route via the SP toward the final destination. (Bob Larson)

Furthermore, when such events would take place, SP units would lead the CZ because WP units were not equipped for the SP signal systems.

This photo was several stories. A derailment on the WP has forced both 17 and 18 to divert over the SP on Saturday, May 27, 1967. In this case, WP's 18 is operating as SP's Passenger Extra 6401 East, and is meeting WP's 17, which is running as SP's Passenger Extra 6443 West at Roseville, California. The 6443 has already slid by the 6401 as the photo was snapped. (Author's Collection)

The CZ was not always simply handled by F units. Switch engines also played a role in the operation of this world wide famous train. In this case, WP Alco S2 No. 554 puts on the finishing touches for train 18 at Oakland on Saturday morning, June 18, 1966. The Dome Observation Sleeping Car, the Silver Horizon, is being reattached to the train after a Pennsylvania Railroad "Pullman" sleeping car had been added to the consist. It was still common in 1966 to find various Eastern Railroads' Pullman cars in the consist of the CZ for special tours, etc. However, the frequency dropped to virtually zero by 1969. (Author's Collection)

Here is a photo of the interior of the California Zephyr Dome Coaches. The coach seat sections were on the main floor level, while the spacious restrooms were located beneath the dome. (Burlington Route Photo, Author's Collection)

Interior of the 16 Section Pullman Sleeping cars assigned to the California Zephyr. The cars could accommodate 32 passengers with the made up lower and upper berths. Otherwise, during the day each section could seat four passengers. Note the leg room in the section to the right with the dad proudly pointing out the spectacular scenery to his daughter. Mom is in the seat facing the two delighted passengers. (Burlington Route Photo, Author's Collection)

Map of the CALIFORNIA ZEPHYR route.

TAKE THE TIME TO LIVE A LITTLE....
......TRAVEL BY TRAIN

See the wonders of America . . . at eye-level.
Avoid highway hazards by dependable "All-Weather" train travel in relaxed comfort.

GENERAL INFORMATION—Please read

RESPONSIBILITY: An earnest and reasonable effort is made to insure accuracy in publishing and maintaining schedules as shown. No responsibility is assumed for possible errors in time-tables, nor for inconvenience or damage resulting from delayed trains or failure to make connections, such matters generally being due to conditions beyond our control. Schedules, equipment and all other information contained herein subject to change without notice.

TIME: From 12:01 midnight to 12:00 Noon is shown by LIGHT faced figures and from **12:01 Noon to 12:00 Midnight by HEAVY faced figures.** LOCAL TIME is used throughout this folder and is referred to as (PT) Pacific Time; (MT) Mountain Time or (CT) Central Time, as the case may be.

ADJUSTMENT OF FARES: In cases of misunderstanding or dis-agreement with conductors or ticket agents, please pay fare requested securing receipt and communicate details to Director of Passenger Sales, 526 Mission Street, San Francisco, Calif. 94105.

REDUCED FARE TICKET RESTRICTIONS: Tickets bearing en-dorsements such as Charity, Clergy, DVS, VAH or Blind and Attendant, will not be honored on the CALIFORNIA ZEPHYR (17 and 18) during the periods June 15 to September 15, in-clusive, and December 15 to January 15, inclusive of each year.

CHECKED BAGGAGE

DEFINITION—Wearing apparel, toilet articles (except liquids) and personal effects, necessary and appropriate for personal use of passenger on journey. Does not include articles prohibited by tariff, such as money, jewelry, silverware, negotiable papers, and like valuables, liquids, fragile or perishable articles, radios, household goods, etc.

Corrugated paper boxes, rope tied, used for personal baggage, must not exceed fifty pounds in weight.

GENERAL INFORMATION—Continued

DOGS, CATS or small household pets (other than Guide or Leader dog) which passengers desire to carry with them in Pullman space must be transported by the passenger between San Fran-cisco and Oakland Depot. Our Trans-Bay Motor Coach service cannot handle these items.

RED CAP SERVICE—SAN FRANCISCO: Passengers departing from San Francisco may check their hand baggage directly to out-going space on the California Zephyr.
Passengers destined San Francisco may check their hand baggage from their space on the California Zephyr directly to cab stand at San Francisco station at a charge of 25c per piece to porter on train.

BAGGAGE PROTECTION: The company's liability for baggage is limited. Like all valuables, your baggage should be protected. Insurance is your best safeguard.
St. Paul Fire & Marine Insurance Company Policies are avail-able at Western Pacific ticket offices.

LOST ARTICLES: Inquiries regarding lost articles and baggage prob-lems should be addressed to Max A. Potter, Chief, Baggage & Rate Bureau, San Francisco, Calif.

FAMILY PLAN BARGAIN FARES!
Take the family on your next trip aboard the Vista-Dome California Zephyr and stretch your travel dollar. Consult your Western Pacific Ticket Agent or Travel Agent for details of how your family can travel at money-saving fares.

FOR ADDITIONAL INFORMATION, please write Robert E. Gonsalves, Director of Passenger Sales, 526 Mission Street, San Francisco, Calif. 94105.

An example of Time Tables issued at the end of the California Zephyr Era.
(Western Pacific, January 1, 1969)

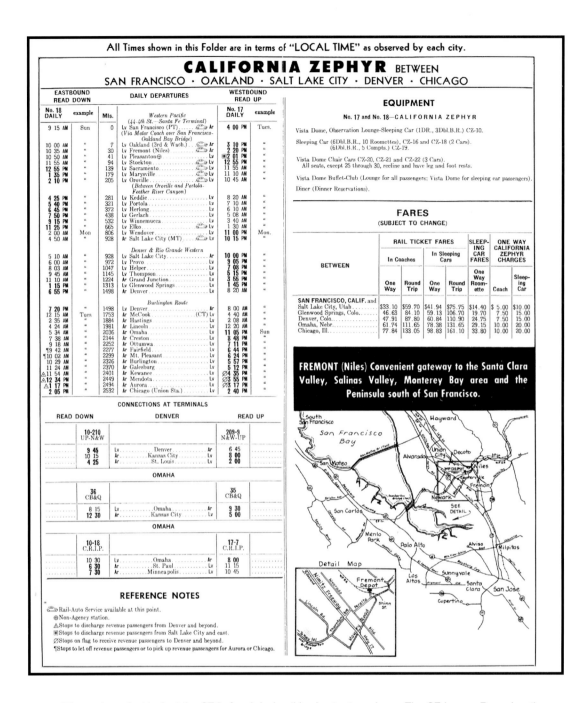

CALIFORNIA ZEPHYR BETWEEN
SAN FRANCISCO · OAKLAND · SALT LAKE CITY · DENVER · CHICAGO

EASTBOUND READ DOWN			DAILY DEPARTURES	WESTBOUND READ UP	
No. 18 DAILY	example	Mls.		No. 17 DAILY	example
			Western Pacific (44-4th St.—Santa Fe Terminal)		
9 15 AM	Sun	0	Lv San Francisco (PT) ... Ar	4 00 PM	Tues.
			(Via Motor Coach over San Francisco-Oakland Bay Bridge)		
10 00 AM	"	7	Lv Oakland (3rd & Wash.) ... Ar	3 10 PM	"
10 35 AM	"	30	Lv Fremont (Niles) ... Ar	2 20 PM	"
10 50 AM	"	41	Lv Pleasanton⊕ ... Lv	2 01 PM	"
11 55 AM	"	94	Lv Stockton ... Lv	12 55 PM	"
12 55 PM	"	139	Lv Sacramento ... Lv	11 55 AM	"
1 35 PM	"	179	Lv Marysville ... Lv	11 10 AM	"
2 10 PM	"	205	Lv Oroville ... Lv	10 45 AM	"
			(Between Oroville and Portola-Feather River Canyon)		
4 25 PM	"	281	Lv Keddie ... Lv	8 20 AM	"
5 40 PM	"	321	Lv Portola ... Lv	7 10 AM	"
6 45 PM	"	372	Lv Herlong ... Lv	6 10 AM	"
7 50 PM	"	438	Lv Gerlach ... Lv	5 08 AM	"
9 15 PM	"	532	Lv Winnemucca ... Lv	3 40 AM	"
11 25 PM	"	665	Lv Elko ... Lv	1 30 AM	"
2 00 AM	Mon	806	Lv Wendover ... Lv	11 00 PM	Mon.
4 50 AM	"	928	Ar Salt Lake City (MT) ... Lv	10 15 PM	"
			Denver & Rio Grande Western		
5 10 AM	"	928	Lv Salt Lake City ... Ar	10 00 PM	"
6 00 AM	"	972	Lv Provo ... Lv	9 05 PM	"
8 03 AM	"	1047	Lv Helper ... Lv	7 08 PM	"
9 45 AM	"	1145	Lv Thompson ... Lv	5 15 PM	"
11 10 AM	"	1224	Ar Grand Junction ... Lv	3 55 PM	"
1 15 PM	"	1313	Ar Glenwood Springs ... Lv	1 45 PM	"
6 55 PM	"	1498	Ar Denver ... Lv	8 20 AM	"
			Burlington Route		
7 20 PM	Tues	1498	Lv Denver ... Ar	8 00 AM	"
12 15 AM	Tues	1753	Lv McCook (CT) Lv	4 40 AM	"
2 35 AM		1884	Ar Hastings ... Lv	2 08 AM	"
4 24 AM		1981	Ar Lincoln ... Lv	12 20 AM	"
5 34 AM		2036	Ar Omaha ... Lv	11 05 PM	Sun
7 38 AM		2144	Ar Creston ... Lv	8 48 PM	"
9 18 AM		2252	Ar Ottumwa ... Lv	7 11 PM	"
¶9 42 AM		2277	Ar Fairfield ... Lv	6 44 PM	"
¶10 02 AM		2299	Ar Mt. Pleasant ... Lv	6 24 PM	"
10 29 AM		2326	Ar Burlington ... Lv	5 57 PM	"
11 24 AM		2370	Ar Galesburg ... Lv	5 12 PM	"
△11 54 AM		2401	Ar Kewanee ... Lv	∅4 35 PM	"
△12 34 PM		2449	Ar Mendota ... Lv	∅3 55 PM	"
△1 17 PM		2494	Ar Aurora ... Lv	∅3 17 PM	"
2 05 PM		2532	Ar Chicago (Union Sta.) ... Lv	2 40 PM	"

EQUIPMENT
No. 17 and No. 18—CALIFORNIA ZEPHYR

Vista Dome, Observation Lounge-Sleeping Car (1DR., 3Dbl.B.R.) CZ-10.

Sleeping Car (6Dbl.B.R., 10 Roomettes), CZ-16 and CZ-18 (2 Cars).
(6Dbl.B.R., 5 Compts.) CZ-19.

Vista Dome Chair Cars CZ-20, CZ-21 and CZ-22 (3 Cars).
All seats, except 25 through 30, recline and have leg and foot rests.

Vista Dome Buffet-Club (Lounge for all passengers; Vista Dome for sleeping car passengers).

Diner (Dinner Reservations).

FARES
(SUBJECT TO CHANGE)

BETWEEN	RAIL TICKET FARES				SLEEPING CAR FARES	ONE WAY CALIFORNIA ZEPHYR CHARGES	
	In Coaches		In Sleeping Cars				
	One Way	Round Trip	One Way	Round Trip	One Way Roomette	Coach	Sleeping Car
SAN FRANCISCO, CALIF. and							
Salt Lake City, Utah	$33.10	$59.70	$41.94	$75.75	$14.40	$ 5.00	$10.00
Glenwood Springs, Colo.	46.63	84.10	59.13	106.70	19.70	7.50	15.00
Denver, Colo.	47.91	87.80	60.84	110.90	24.75	7.50	15.00
Omaha, Nebr.	61.74	111.65	78.38	131.65	29.15	10.00	20.00
Chicago, Ill.	77.84	133.05	98.83	161.10	33.80	10.00	20.00

FREMONT (Niles) Convenient gateway to the Santa Clara Valley, Salinas Valley, Monterey Bay area and the Peninsula south of San Francisco.

CONNECTIONS AT TERMINALS

READ DOWN	DENVER	READ UP
10-210 UP-N&W		209-9 N&W-UP
9 45	Lv ... Denver ... Ar	6 45
10 15	Ar ... Kansas City ... Lv	8 00
4 25	Ar ... St. Louis ... Lv	2 00

	OMAHA	
36 CB&Q		35 CB&Q
8 15	Lv ... Omaha ... Ar	9 30
12 30	Ar ... Kansas City ... Lv	5 00

	OMAHA	
10-18 C.R.I.P.		17-7 C.R.I.P.
10 30	Lv ... Omaha ... Ar	8 00
6 30	Ar ... St. Paul ... Lv	11 15
7 30	Ar ... Minneapolis ... Lv	10 45

REFERENCE NOTES

Rail-Auto Service available at this point.
⊕ Non-Agency station.
△ Stops to discharge revenue passengers from Denver and beyond.
⊠ Stops to discharge revenue passengers from Salt Lake City and east.
∅ Stops on flag to receive revenue passengers to Denver and beyond.
¶ Stops to let off revenue passengers or to pick up revenue passengers for Aurora or Chicago.

We need one last look at the CZ before bringing this chapter to a close. The CZ is near Reno Junction with the 805A doing the honors. A steam generator car follows the two units on this 10 car train in January, 1970. (Collection of Lou Schmitz)

Chapter 5

THE ZEPHYRETTE

Following World War II, the Western Pacific was faced with rising passenger train costs, and the daily local trains 1 and 2, either in the form of the Feather River Express, or the Royal Gorge, was simply too much train service between Salt Lake City and Oakland. In fact, the conventional trains on this particular run cost the WP nearly $900,000 in 1949. (1)

Obviously this could not go on, but at the same time, the situation was not completely hopeless, and the WP made the decision to up-grade the service with Rail Diesel Cars, and simultaneously place the operation on a tri-weekly basis. Two RDC-2s were ordered from the Budd Company, and delivered during the summer of 1950. The change in service and the new equipment reduced the WP's operating costs of running 1 and 2 by over $650,000. It was a wise decision indeed for the year 1950.

The WP RDCs were slightly different from the normal off the shelf sales of such equipment. First off, the WP removed the 22 commuter style seats from the forward coach section of the car, and replaced them with 18 reclining seats. RDC-2s were normally equipped with only one washroom, but the WP added a women's washroom on the left side of the forward section, known as coach section "A." The single seat at the rear of the coach section "B" was transformed into a conductor's office space. In addition, the car received number boards above the vestibules and the name Zephyrette was painted on the sides next to the baggage doors. It was a sharp RDC car to say the least.

The two cars went into service on September 15, 1950 on a tri-weekly basis departing the end terminals on Sunday, Wednesday and Friday. No. 1 departed Salt Lake City at 8:30 a.m. Mountain time (7:30 Pacific) and arrived at Oakland, 3rd and Washington Depot at

6:50 a.m. the next morning. Passengers arrived at the Ferry Building in San Francisco at 7:35 a.m. Eastbound passengers departed San Francisco at 7:30 p.m., the Oakland depot at 8:08 p.m. Pacific time, and arrived at Salt Lake City at 7:45 p.m. Mountain time the next evening.

Throughout the 1950s, the RDCs provided local passenger, mail and express service along the 928 mile main line. However, one could not expect the decade to slip by without changes. By the time eight years had passed, service between San Francisco and Oakland had been discontinued, but the trains still ran their tri-weekly schedule. However, running times had been speeded up. According to the September 28, 1958 time table, No. 2 made the trip in 21 hours, 45 minutes; while No. 1 scooted across the main line in 21 hours, 25 minutes. (2) Although running times were slow compared to the schedule of the CZ, they were actually very tight considering a 30 minute meal stop at Elko and Portola, and the fact that 50 stops were made between Salt Lake City and Oakland. However, 23 of these were flag stops.

The trains during their early careers averaged about 38 passengers per trip. Most of these were local in nature, and the trains handled very few through Oakland - Salt Lake City passengers. As one might guess, the patronage fig-

The Zephyrette: What a superb name for a "Rail Diesel Car." The name fit perfectly, especially in view of the California Zephyr's popularity and notoriety. Although the RDC-2 was practically an "off-the-shelf" purchase from the Budd Company, the car did carry number boards as well as the name "Zephyrette" just behind the baggage door. The 376 was photographed running as train No. 2 at Elko, Nevada on New Years Eve, December 31, 1959. (Author's Collection)

ure dropped as more and more automobiles populated the Zephyrette's route. The trains also handled a small amount of Railway Express Business, most of which was eastbound from Oakland to Portola, and local locked pouches of mail. In both cases, this business dwindled away. Trains 1 and 2 also handled a substantial amount of railroad company mail.

By 1960, operating costs were up substantially from what they were in 1950, with revenues sinking fast, the WP was faced with the unhappy task of requesting the abandonment of service. Their economic usefulness was simply outlived, and train 1 and 2 finally went the way of all local trains in the west, and disappeared from the time tables. These tri-weekly trains were the last of the local services to be ever operated by the WP - but what a glorious little train: THE ZEPHYRETTE!

Complete Main Line Schedules showing trains 1 and 2, the Zephyrette. (Western Pacific Railroad Time Tables, September 30, 1951, page 2.)

No. 2 Zephyrette Leaves Sun Wed Fri	No. 18 California Zephyr Daily	Miles	COMPLETE MAIN LINE SCHEDULES	Elevation	No. 17 California Zephyr Daily	No. 1 Zephyrette Arrives Mon Thur Sat
7 30	9 00	0	Lv (PT) San Francisco (Ferry Bldg.) (PT) Ar		4 50	7 35
7 50	9 20	4	Ar........Oakland Pier........Lv	14	4 30	7 15
7 57	9 26	4	Lv........Oakland Pier........Ar	14	4 15	7 05
8 08	9 37	7	Lv....Oakland (3rd & Washington)....Ar	18	4 02	6 50
f8 39		20	Lv........Hayward........Lv	99		f6 15
f8 52	Ⓐ10 16	30	Lv........Niles........Lv	68	Ⓑ 3 18	f6 02
f9 03		41	Lv........Pleasanton........Lv	341		f5 45
f9 19		48	Lv........Livermore........Lv	480		f5 35
		57	Lv........Altamont........Lv	752		
10 21	11 35	94	Lv........Stockton........Lv	22	1 54	4 34
10 23	11 37	94	Lv........Stockton........Ar	22	1 52	4 32
		105	Lv........Kingdon........Lv	27		
10 48		114	Lv........Thornton........Lv	20		4 06
		136	Lv........South Sacramento........Lv	28		
11 27	12 33	139	Lv........Sacramento........Lv	23	12 55	3 28
		156	Lv........Pleasant Grove........Lv	48		
12 19	1 23	179	Lv........Marysville........Lv	86	12 01	2 30
12 55	1 55	205	Lv........Oroville........Lv	203	11 33	1 55
1 00	2 05	205	Ar........Oroville........Ar	203	11 25	1 50
f1 34		221	Lv........Las Plumas........Lv	560		f1 10
f1 40		224	Lv........Berry Creek........Lv	693		f1 03
f1 53		230	Lv........Isaiah........Lv	990		f12 49
f1 55		231	Lv........David........Lv	986		f12 47
f2 14		239	Lv........Pulga........Lv	1380		f12 27
f2 18		241	Lv........Mayaro........Lv	1451		f12 21
f2 22		244	Lv........Cresta........Lv	1580		f12 15
f2 30		248	Lv........Merlin........Lv	1758		f12 05
f2 43		253	Lv........Tobin........Lv	2006		f11 52
f2 48		256	Lv........Camp Rodgers........Lv	2128		f11 46
2 59		260	Lv........Belden........Lv	2306		11 35
f3 08		265	Lv........Rich Bar........Lv	2502		f11 24
f3 19		270	Lv........Virgilia........Lv	2752		f11 10
f3 27		274	Lv........Twain........Lv	2909		f11 02
f3 34		278	Lv........Paxton........Lv	3080		f10 54
3 46	f4 20	281	Lv........Keddie........Lv	3227	f9 12	10 45
f3 56		285	Lv....Spanish Creek (Oak. Mun. Camp)....Lv	3432		f10 32
4 07		288	Lv....Quincy Junction....Lv	3545		10 27
f4 15		292	Lv........Massack........Lv	3759		f10 17
f4 22		297	Lv........Spring Garden........Lv	3964		f10 10
f4 32		302	Lv........Sloat........Lv	4117		10 00
f4 40		306	Lv........Two Rivers........Lv	4260		f9 53
		309	Lv........Feather River Inn........Lv	4359		9 46
4 50		310	Lv........Blairsden........Lv	4414		9 44
f4 59		314	Lv........Clio........Lv	4577		f9 34
||5 15	5 25	321	Ar........Portola........Lv	4834	8 05	||9 20
||5 45	5 28	321	Lv........Portola........Ar	4834	8 02	||8 40
f5 55		328	Lv........Hawley........Lv	4875		f8 28
f6 07		339	Lv........Chilcoot........Lv	5003		f8 14
f6 11		342	Lv........Reno Junction........Lv	4986		f8 08
6 42		363	Lv........Doyle........Lv	4262		f7 35
7 05	6 25	372	Lv........Herlong........Lv	4119	7 05	7 17
f7 30		394	Lv........Sand Pass........Lv	4199		f6 47
8 19	7 35	438	Lv........Gerlach........Lv	3931	5 57	5 57
f8 55		475	Lv........Sulphur........Lv	4042		f5 15
f9 20		497	Lv........Jungo........Lv	4167		f4 50
9 55	9 05	532	Ar........Winnemucca........Lv	4334	4 28	4 15
10 00	9 12	532	Lv........Winnemucca........Ar	4334	4 21	4 00
f10 18		548	Lv........Golconda........Lv	4346		f3 35
		589	Lv........Battle Mountain........Lv	4501		2 50
f11 37		620	Lv........Beowawe........Lv	4631		f2 15
f12 12		645	Lv........Carlin........Lv	4899		1 40
||12 45	11 15	665	Ar........Elko........Lv	5061	2 15	||1 15
||1 15	11 17	665	Lv........Elko........Ar	5061	2 13	||12 45
f1 54		700	Lv........Deeth........Lv	5341		f12 06
2 15		718	Lv........Wells........Lv	5631		11 43
3 15		767	Lv........Shafter........Lv	5594		10 50
f3 59		789	Lv........Pilot........Lv	6138		f10 16
4 15	f	806	Ar........Wendover........Lv	4246	f	9 50
4 25	f	806	Ar........Wendover........Ar	4246	f	9 45
f5 36		878	Lv........Delle........Lv	4270		f8 33
f5 57		897	Lv........Burmester........Lv	4224		f8 12
f6 16		913	Lv..(PT)......Garfield......(PT)..Lv	4232		f7 54
7 45	5 20	928	Ar..(MT)....Salt Lake City....(MT)..Lv	4233	10 40	8 30
Arrives Mon Thur Sat	Daily		Ⓐ Stops to discharge revenue passengers from Salt Lake City and east. Ⓑ Stops on flag to pick up revenue passengers for Salt Lake City and east.		Daily	Leaves Sun Wed Fri

Endnotes:

1. W. H. Hutchinson, "A Streetcar Named Zephyrette," TRAINS, July, 1952, p. 26.
2. Western Pacific Passenger Train Time Table, September 28, 1958.

Another view of the No. 376, this time at the Zephyrette's station stop at Winnemucca, Nevada. (Collection of Lou Schmitz)

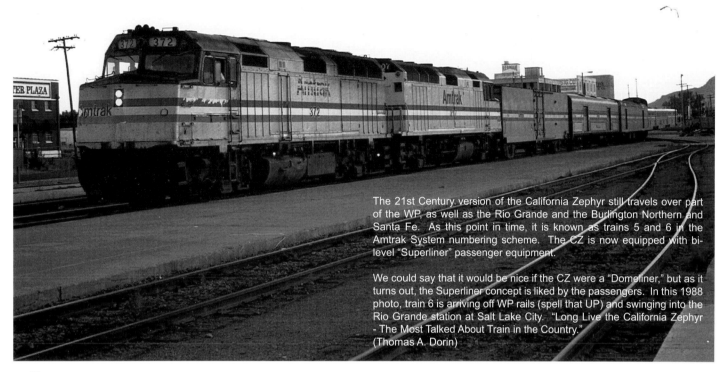

The 21st Century version of the California Zephyr still travels over part of the WP, as well as the Rio Grande and the Burlington Northern and Santa Fe. As this point in time, it is known as trains 5 and 6 in the Amtrak System numbering scheme. The CZ is now equipped with bi-level "Superliner" passenger equipment.

We could say that it would be nice if the CZ were a "Domeliner," but as it turns out, the Superliner concept is liked by the passengers. In this 1988 photo, train 6 is arriving off WP rails (spell that UP) and swinging into the Rio Grande station at Salt Lake City. "Long Live the California Zephyr - The Most Talked About Train in the Country."
(Thomas A. Dorin)

Chapter 6

AMTRAK & THE ALTAMONT COMMUTER EXPRESS

The Western Pacific did not participate in the original operation of any Amtrak passenger train. However, Amtrak's San Francisco Zephyr was listed in the Western Pacific's Division time tables as SP PSGR 6 (meaning Southern Pacific Passenger train 6) in the joint trackage area between Weso and Alazon. (1)

When the Rio Grande began operation of the Superliner California Zephyr between Denver and Salt Lake City, the former Western Pacific tracks between Salt lake City and Alazon became the home of the CZ once again. Thus the former Feather River Division is not a freight only section of the railroad, and what better name to grace the WP rails than "California Zephyr." (2)

It is a bit hard to believe but the WP trackage that is now part of the Union Pacific hosts passenger train services - in fact as of this writing, three trains in each direction between Niles and Lathrop. This is part of the new Altamont Commuter Express train services between Stockton and San Jose,

which is part of California's solution to the severe highway congestion and pollution problems. (Other states need to study California's new passenger train services.) The ACE's equipment and motive power are serviced and maintained at the former WP facilities in Stockton. Thus one can ride UP's Western Pacific trackage with all new train services in 2006. Still another way to enjoy the WP, life and travel for real by rail.

Endnotes:

1. Western Pacific Time Table, No. 1, June 11, 1972.
2. Amtrak Time Table, Summer, 2001.

As we moved into the late 1990s and the 21st Century, there is now a new passenger train operating on the former WP rails. The Altamont Commuter Express, which began service in 1998, runs between Stockton and San Jose with operations over the former WP trackage between Niles and Lathrop. (Wayne Monger, ACE)

This photo shows an eastbound ACE train at Livermore on April 30, 1999. The train to the left in the siding in Union Pacific 6273 West. (Bob Larson)

Chapter 7

TONNAGE THROUGH THE FEATHER RIVER CANYON

The bread and butter of the North American Railroad System is the freight services. The Western Pacific began freight service as early as 1908 even though the construction was not completed until 1910. The first revenue runs were made between Salt Lake City and Shafter, Nevada, where the company connected with the Nevada Northern Railroad. Except for some local traffic between Salt Lake City and Shafter, most of this business had to do with the copper mining in the Ely-Kimberly area. Overall tonnages were small in those early days, but by 1912 when operations were transferred from the construction department to the operating department, the annual tonnage was 1,000,211 tons. From that time until 1917, the annual tonnage did not vary too much or show much promise of growth. However, in 1917 because of World War I, tonnage jumped to 2,329,018 tons. It stayed at that amount until 1921 when traffic fell off to 1.7 million tons. From that time, however, WP traffic began to climb year after year. No spectacular increases, but absolute steady growth!

The Western Pacific joined the Pacific Fruit Express to

Western Pacific freight services have been characterized in several different ways. For example, some people find it very warming to visualize it as mallet steam power pounding their way with tremendous stack music and a long drag.

And this is what we have here. The 252 is rolling east with train 82 bound from Oakland to Salt Lake City, and is shaking the very foundations of the Oroville, California depot. The photo was taken on September 16, 1939. Yet this scene is frozen in time by the true time machine, the camera, and it will exist as long as the negatives, photographs, and perhaps even this book continue to remain in decent physical condition. (Bill Pennington Photo, Bob Larson Collection)

secure an improved refrigerator car supply in 1924. The PFE was owned by the Southern Pacific and the Union Pacific.

Traffic continued to improve through the middle and late 1920s, and it reached nearly 4 million tons in 1928 and 1929. It slipped only a little in 1930, the first year of the Great Depression. The tonnage that year amounted to 3,775,597 but by 1933 - traffic fell by more than 33% when the total tonnage carried was 2,756,672. From that time business began to pick up again and a record tonnage was handled in 1937 with 4,183,136 tons.

The railroad was very much aware in 1930 that business was going to slip away. However, no one at that point could predict how long the Depression would last. In an effort to prevent the loss of traffic, the Western Pacific worked out a joint agreement with the Union Pacific and Burlington Railroads for faster perishable freight service. In May of 1930, the three railroads announced that 24 hours would be cut from the transit time on perishables from Central and Northern California to Chicago. This meant seventh morning delivery instead of eight in Chicago. In order to accomplish this faster schedule, a new routing was set up. Previously, the traffic moved via the WP to Salt Lake City, the Rio Grande to Denver, and the Burlington to Chicago. The new routing beyond WP trackage was the Union Pacific Salt Lake City to Sidney, Nebraska, and the Burlington Route beyond to Chicago. This amounted to a savings in mileage of nearly 300 miles. (1)

One must remember that this savings in miles was before the Rio Grande completed the Dotsero cut-off in 1934. That cut-off shortened the Rio Grande's Denver - Salt Lake City main line by 175 miles.

With the drop in both passenger and freight business on the branch lines, the WP was faced with the problem of how to reduce train miles without reducing service. Or shall we say, with a minimum reduction in service. By 1935, the company had discontinued passenger trains on all of the branch lines. They also substituted mixed train services (passenger and freight) on the Calpine, Loyalton, and Reno branches. Trains 313 and 314 operated tri-weekly on the Calpine branch. Train 415 and 416 were also tri-weekly operations on the Loyalton branch, while the Reno branch merited a daily train service. All of these

Another mallet, No. 207, a 2-6-6-2, is moving through the snow. The pilot mounted plow will help as this freight moves through the Sierra Nevada Mountains. (TLC Collection)

branches were handled through operations out of Portola.

All of the trains carried a combination coach and baggage car for the few passengers and express shipments. Unfortunately, the branch line mixed train services did not connect with main line passenger train, the Scenic Limited, which was at the time the only passenger service on the WP. (2)

Truck competition became an increasing threat as time approached the 1940s. In order to meeting this competition, the company inaugurated a Merchandise Dispatch Service on March 28, 1941 between San Francisco and Sacramento, Marysville, Oroville, Chico, Yuba City, and points on the Colusa Branch of the Sacramento Northern Railroad. The service provided overnight early first morning delivery of freight at points in the Sacramento Valley served either directly by the Western Pacific or in conjunction with the Sacramento Northern.

Fifteen freight cars, converted for Less-Than-Carload-Lot-Service in the company shops, were used in a pool for the service. (3) Also by 1941, business on the whole was picking up but no one had any idea of the volume the WP would be called upon to handle for World War II..

As soon as hostilities broke out, the WP felt the increase. In 1942, traffic was more than 100% higher than it had been in 1938. This increase required numerous additions to not only train and station services, but also to the operating department supervisory forces. This was done primarily to increase car and locomotive utilization. (4) To complicate matters even more, train movements had to be kept fluid at all times.

With both a freight car and locomotive shortage, this was often very difficult. The average tonnage per train jumped from less than 900 in 1941 to over 1,118 tons in 1942. The additional tonnage, however, had its effect on train speed which dropped from an average of 19.8 miles per hour in 1941 to 16.6 in

1942. This reduction was not all due to increased train tonnage for some of it was attributable to longer delays during train meets and passes on sidings because of the greater number of trains being operated on the single track main line. (5)

As with the other transcontinental railroads, the WP had to revise its operations since the war reversed the normal direction of the predominant loaded movements. Up until the war, the heavier loadings had been eastbound. The same situation existed with the Southern Pacific's main line from Oakland to Ogden. Under the stress of the getting the war time traffic from Salt Lake City or Ogden to the West Coast, the SP and the WP began working together. (6) War time tonnage reached its highest point in 1945 with a total of 10,249,448 tons. When the war ended, it began to slide downward but not as drastically as one might have thought.

Peacetime tonnages slipped to approximately 6.5 million tons in 1949. The Korean War kicked it back up again to over 8 million tons in 1952. A tonnage very similar to the years 1942, 1946 and 1947. Overall freight tonnage would increase, with some dips, steadily for the next twenty years.

No one really expected the United States and its economy to forge ahead after the war, but it did. Part of this was the aide that was sent to Asia and Europe after the war destruction. The WP geared itself to the expanding economy and went after freight traffic vigorously and worked to retain it.

The company began a new signaling program in 1948 that eventually placed Centralized Traffic Control over the entire main line by 1953. (7) From the moment the CTC began to be placed in operation, the on-time performance of

The Pulga Bridge looms bright and neat in a photograph taken from the top of the tank of a 2-8-8-2 heading up a westbound fast freight No. 53 en route from Roper Yard to Oakland Yard. The Pulga bridge is on the Third Subdivision of the Western Division. (Bill Pennington, Bob Larson Collection)

WP No. 257 leads an eastbound freight train through the canyon near the entrance to Keddie Yard in this 1947 scene. (TLC Collection)

freight trains improved substantially - a factor that contributed to the increase in traffic over the years.

With the improvements in freight train performance and service on the main line, the WP turned its efforts to the Northern California Extension from Keddie to Bieber. As the reader will recall from Chapter 1, the Bieber line was part of the middle segment of a north-south line between Southern California and the Pacific Northwest consisting of the Great Northern, Santa Fe, and the WP. In 1949 the three railroads began to make plans to improve service on the "Inside Gateway."

The presidents, traffic and operating officers of the three railroads went on a week long barnstorming trip in 1950 calling at Seattle, Tacoma, Portland, Klamath Falls, Oregon, San Francisco and Los Angeles. The trip had three goals. One was to publicize and promote the "Gateway." Another was to make the officers of each railroad familiar with those portions of the route on the "other railroads." Finally, and most important, the trip became a striking and unusual means by which the officers of the three lines, with widely separated headquarters, could settle in person the manifold details of establishing a new faster, more reliable freight service over a route from Vancouver, British Columbia to San Diego, California.

In addition to meeting with shippers, the special train of five business and lounge cars, became the locale of separate

conferences of departmental officers. In one car, operating men looked over past performances on the route to determine what would be necessary to provide a better service. In another business car, the traffic officers wrote out their prescription of what would be necessary to win business over, especially traffic over the highways. (8)

When the separate groups arrived at conclusions, a joint meeting was held in the Great Northern lounge car where a plan was developed for presentation to the company presidents. As the special train passed between Klamath Falls and Bieber, over the link which made the "Inside Gateway" possible, the final plan was set forth and the presidents gave it their approval. (9)

The plan was announced to the public in February, 1950. The faster service shaved 24 hours off the previous schedules between Washington points and Southern California. Under the new schedule, two freight trains were operated each way over the 1,484 mile route on a daily basis. (10) The running time of the four regular scheduled trains was approximately 100 hours.

Although the improved service placed in operation in early 1950 drew additional traffic, the three railroads were still not entirely satisfied. The 1950 schedules provided "4th Afternoon" or "5th Morning" delivery. In 1953, the running times of the four trains were reduced by as much as 13 hours which allowed fourth morning delivery in either Los Angeles or Seattle. The maximum running time of any of the trains was 84 hours. (11) Expedited and more efficient switching at intermediate terminals also contributed to the time savings.

During this same time period after the War, the WP was running three freights each way daily over the main line. Running times were approximately 36 to 44 hours for

Another example of the rugged terrain as the 257 begins the crossing of the Keddie Wye bridge. (TLC Collection)

The Western Pacific provided a wide variety of freight services for shippers. This photo shows a special stock train near Portola, California in 1947. (TLC Collection)

the entire distance between Oakland and Salt Lake City. For example, train 77 departed Roper Yard at Salt Lake City at 8:00 p.m. It passed through Portola at 5:00 p.m. the next afternoon, and arrived in Oakland at 4:00 o'clock the second afternoon. (12) The total time between terminals was 44 hours. The three freight trains were scheduled to depart the end terminals approximately 8 hours apart. In addition to the three time freights, the WP operated as many as six extra trains in each direction. Most of this traffic consisted of perishables going east or solid trains empty refrigerator cars moving to the California growing areas.

The year 1954 brought further improvements in WP freight train services. Westbound main line freights, for example the California Freight Special (CFS), were speeded up by approximately five to seven hours. This was made possible by the completion of the CTC system mentioned previously. Also with the CTC system, it was no longer necessary to give the train time table schedules as "Second Class" trains. (Passengers trains were usually run as "First Class" trains.) The WP operated the main line freights as "Extra" trains since the dispatcher had finger tip control over the trains. Previous to CTC, when a train was able to run ahead of its time table schedule, the crew had to stop and call the dispatcher and let him know the conditions governing their train. If other train traffic was in position on the railroad that permitted the crew to run ahead of time, the dispatcher would have to annul the train, and issue new train orders for the crew to run "extra." With CTC the dispatcher was (is) aware of all traffic conditions by just looking at the track diagram board. A train can be moved across a division or subdivision as fast as possible consistent with safety. Thus with CTC and improved switching techniques at intermediate yards, such as Portola, the WP was moving freight trains very fast over their main line. For example, the PBF rolled from Roper Yard to Oakland in 26 hours. PBF departed Salt Lake City at 8:30 p.m., passed Portola at 10:30 a.m. the next morning and arrived in Oakland at 10:30 p.m. (13) This was the type of scheduling that brought the WP into the 1960s.

Meanwhile things hadn't been exactly standing still on the "Inside Gateway." In late 1954, the WP and GN sought to speed up service even faster. Eight

hours were shaved off the running time of symbol freight SWG. The train departed Oakland at 10:00 p.m. and arrived at Seattle at 10:00 p.m. the second evening - 48 hours later. The schedule provided ample time for Great Northern switch crews to place loads for third morning delivery to Seattle industries. (14) The following year a new joint piggyback train was placed in service between Los Angeles and the Pacific Northwest. Trailers were handled on the new tri-weekly "Expediter" which departed Southern California points on Monday, Tuesday and Friday. Trailers on other days of the week ran on the SWG. (15)

Mixed train services had been totally discontinued by 1950. As the reader will recall, the WP had operated three sets of mixed trains. In 1947, only the tri-weekly Loyalton branch train was still serving passengers.

Although not widely known, there were still other Western Pacific freight trains that were authorized to carry passengers. These were the trains on the "Inside Gateway." Since very few people took advantage of the service, the California Public Utilities Commission authorized the discontinuance of the applicable tariffs on passengers riding freight trains on that line on October 26, 1959. Passengers were permitted to ride the caboose, but only 145 did so between 1953 and 1959. One may wonder how it was that particular line offered passenger service on freight trains. When the original plans were made for construction of the "Inside Gateway," one of the items put forth to the ICC to convince them to give their blessings to the project was that the Great Northern's Empire Builder would operate to Oakland. Since the Depression precluded that operation, passenger service was provided by freight trains for those people who wished to take advantage of the service. The year 1959 was the last one for any passenger service on freight trains on the "Inside Gateway."

Mikado No. 325, a 2-8-2, is handling the first section of an eastbound time freight near Oroville, California. Although the identity is not 100% certain, this appears to be the first section (green flags) of time freight 54 based on the angle of the early morning sunlight. No 54 was due into Oroville at 8:30 a.m. on its run from Oakland to Salt Lake City. (TLC Collection)

From 1950 to 1959, the annual tonnages on the WP hovered around the 7 to 8 million mark. Early in 1959, the company conducted a study to determine potential markets and decided to go after them. It was with great vigor and vitality that the Traffic Department and Mr. Whitman, the WP's president, announced to North American shippers and industry the railroad's tool of the trade. RAIL-WAY AGE reported three of the biggest guns as follows: (16)

1. Schedules between the Midwest and the West Coast were as fast or faster in some cases than the trucks.

2. A modern freight car fleet with heavy emphasis on special purpose cars. Mr. Whitman pointed out that the average age of WP freight cars was 12 years (in 1959) compared with the national average of 19 years. At that time, 21% or 1,118 cars of the WP's fleet were special purpose cars.

3. Western Pacific joined "Trailer Train."

White flags on the other hand indicated an extra train. In this case, it is Extra 256 East with a drag freight near Quartz, California on the Third Subdivision of the Western Division. The photo was taken in June, 1947, and the WP has already installed Centralized Traffic Control between Quartz (6.4 miles east of Oroville Yard) and Delleker (1.36 miles west of Portola). This means that all trains, even though they may be scheduled as First or Second Class Trains in the Division timetable, have no timetable authority, and thus no superiority. Train meets and passes are handled at the discretion of the dispatcher. In reality, the white flags were not necessary in CTC territory. (Bill Pennington, Bob Larson Collection)

With a positive attitude, the WP faced the turbulent 1960s and freight traffic continued its slow but steady climb during that time. The annual tonnages moved from 7,160,576 tons in 1960 to establish a new peace time record for tonnage in 1968 with 9,283,051. The previous peace time record, without the impact of World Wars or the Korean War, was in 1947 with 8,478,315.

Still other changes were in the works. The WP terminated its contract with Pacific Fruit Express, and established a new contract with Fruit Growers Express for the refrigerator car supply on September 30, 1967. (17)

Train operations too came under scrutiny. Increased traffic on the "Inside Gateway" required an additional regular freight train on the line. This meant three fast freights each way daily instead of the previous two. Furthermore, all of these were powered by pooled power with the Great Northern, and later the Burlington Northern.

The Western Pacific also began to run through freight trains with the Union Pacific at Salt Lake City. New operating techniques, such as pre-blocking of trains, paid handsome dividends in time savings. This operating diligence had the effect of retaining shippers and securing new ones, and it also provided the company with an adequate mix of traffic over the years.

Freight train operations were not the only facet undergoing changes during the late 1960s and early 70s. The Western Pacific brought in the computer for car supply and to improve service for shippers. According to an article in the January 26, 1970 issue of RAILWAY AGE, the company connected two computers as the key units in the WP's Management Information and Control Systems.

This early system was known as MICS, and it provided the shipper with instant car tracing, information, and better distribution of empty cars for loading. The car distribution system was implemented in early 1969. The tracing system, which was known as CLICS, meaning Car Location Information Computer System was also placed into operation during the same year. Still another aspect of this system provided complete waybill data upon inquiry to the computer. The fourth phase tied all of the other phases together to provide planning and forecasting capability to the freight car utilization function.

How did MICS work? First of all, the computer kept records. The car distribution system made use of the computer as a record keeper while strategically placing supervision in the field. The WP set up 11 service regions along the main lines from Oakland to Salt Lake City, and the "Inside Gateway" connection north from Keddie, California to Klamath Falls, Oregon. Each of the 11 regions contained a service center staffed with a regional car distributor.

There were two tenets basic to the car distribution system. First cars were cleaned and inspected at the nearest facility after being unloaded. Second the cars were moved between regions only on specific orders, which came directly from the Superintendent of Transportation's office in San Francisco.

The procedure for making empty cars available for distribution for loading, or for returning empty foreign cars, began when they arrived in the yards following unloading. They were often placed for cleaning. Car inspectors would then enter information about the condition of the cars on special card forms. After inspection and cleaning was completed, the information on the card form would be sent via teletype to the WP computer center in the San Francisco office.

One of the original orange color schemes with green trim graces FT No. 907 (May 20, 1947), on the head-end of train 153 en route from Bieber to Keddie on the Fourth Subdivision of the Western Division. The train has a clear order board at the Crescent Mills train order office, just 8.6 miles from the final destination at Keddie and the connection with the WP's Third Division Main Line. (Bill Pennington, Bob Larson Collection)

The computer itself was programmed to analyze this information and issue a classification for each car. These classifications were in the form of codes that indicated the type of car, its condition, and its availability for loading status. The car type was broken down to indicate size, special loading devices, and other features. The condition of the car, a summary, indicated in general what type of load it could handle, such as lumber, machinery, bulk loads, etc. The availability status also indicated what, if any, restrictions might apply.

The computer automatically sent the car type, condition-summary, and availability status codes to the office sending in the information. This report also included any expectations to general rules that might have applied to the car movement. Upon receipt of this code information, the codes were marked on the card form for the particular car. These forms were put on manila stock measuring 4 1/4 by 11 inches to serve a double purpose: First to provide car condition information and second, to serve, when required, as an empty car waybill moving the car for distribution from one region to another.

The WP designed the computer system in such a way that it would be a benefit for customers. Customers could either call WP agents or sales representatives with requests for cars. The person who received the call would complete the "car order" form that would show the customer's name, assigned patron number, date, and time car required, date and time the order was placed, commodity description, number and type of cars requested. This information was then punched into a paper tape and sent via Teletype to the central computer where a record was made.

The regional car distributors would naturally, try to fill their car orders from cars in the region. When an order was filled, they would notify the central computer via teletype so that the central file was updated. Upon request of the car distributors in the Transportation Center, the computer would prepare a supply and demand report for each of the 11 service regions. Each region would receive via Teletype its own regional report, and the Transportation Department in San Francisco would receive a consolidated report.

The report listed the car supply for the system and included foreign cars in various availability status codes broken down by car type and condition summary codes. On the demand side, the report provided numbers of cars by type and condition summary under five types of orders, such as car orders, distribution orders, surplus orders, standing orders, and finally switch orders.

The car distributors of the Transportation Department would check this report carefully, especially the surplus of cars and orders. They would find a region with a surplus of a particular kind of car, and another region with a surplus of orders for the same type of car. Accordingly, the car distributor would issue a distribution order directing the surplus cars to be moved to the region short of the needed cars. The order would be sent to the computer so that it would update the file on the car inventory for the two regions involved. The Western Pacific gave the same priority to moving empties as it did for moving loads. It did so for two reasons: First to give the shipper better service by promptly fulfilling his car requirements, and secondly, to keep per-diem costs down by promptly moving surplus foreign line empties off line.

An auxiliary report showing which cars to move was also printed by the computer when it prepared the supply and demand report. This report listed cars by railroad initials and number, whether it was a load or empty, car type, availability status, condition summary, car order (if under such an order), location (yard or in a train), date arrived at present location, and finally a "remarks" section. This last category might indicate if a car had been over 72 hours at the same location.

During the 1960s and 70s, more loaded cars terminated

It is June, 1959, and station time at the Keddie depot for train 18, the California Zephyr. Although the CZ has center stage here for the moment, there is much more to this photo than the CZ. No. 18 is actually passing the Westwood Turn, which is in the siding to the left rear. On the right are helper engines in the form of GP7s and/or 9s. The action here on this bright, sunny day is involving three separate train and engine movements. (Bob Larson)

on the Western Pacific than originated. Therefore, this 72 hour designation was especially helpful to car distributors for foreign line cars. Kenneth Plummer, WP's Superintendent of Transportation, reported in the RAILWAY AGE article that the company was working toward a 48 hour and 24 hour detention flagging periods for the report. He also commented that the biggest advantage of the MICS was its ability to assist in getting the maximum utilization of freight car equipment, foreign cars could be moved toward their owners with or without loads, and finally the WP maintained control of excessive detention of cars.

The Western Pacific was a pioneer in a modern day concept of "Just-in-Time" freight service. In this case, a two car Ford Special (auto-parts) is departing Stockton on the First Subdivision of the Western Division in CTC Territory - known on the WP as TCS, or Traffic Control System. The photo was taken in July, 1958, when it was very common for the railroads to wait for tonnage. Not so on the WP, the auto parts were needed at the destination - "ON TIME!" A Note to Model Rails - Who says main line freights really have to be long? (Bob Larson)

The MICS System provided for inquiry to the computer for information concerning cars reported on the supply and demand, and auxiliary reports. One example was car location information. Another concerned car utilization. In this case, the computer used the American Association of Railroad UMLER (Universal Machine Language Equipment Register) file in real time. The car type code was developed from UMLER. Thus from any teletype location, five types of inquiry could be handled by the computer: (1) specifications and dimensions of a specific car; (2) listing of the car type code, condition-summary code, availability status code, present location, and condition summary detail; (3) complete listing of a specific car order (This would have to indicate ordering station and order number); (4) list of detail for car utilization; (5) list of last reported location times and dates.

The CLIC, or the Car Location Information Computer System, became operational in July 1969. The train consists

were sent into the computer via teletype and contained such information as train identification number, date and time of the report, and movement record code indicating departure, passing stations, arrival or delivery at a junction (the entire train or for individual cars). At the same time, the report was sent from the originating yard to the next yard and to the computer system. When the cars were reported for the first time, the computer would automatically check them against UMLER for validity. If it did not pass this check, the computer would automatically ask the sending station for a correction. If there were ten or more errors in a train consist, the computer rejected it and asked for a retransmission. Trains passing through yards were reported as well as "bad order" cars and the central file was continuously updated.

Shippers were also kept informed through this system. Car location messages, known CLMs, were sent daily to customers via Western Union Telex Service. Also many of the WP's twelve off-line or six on-line sales offices could inquire via teletype to the computer for car location information. A daily PARD (passing, arrival, delivery) report was mailed to sales offices and representatives not equipped with teletypewriter equipment to assist personnel in car tracing. A computer produced "jumbo" report was also available to the transportation department at the railroad headquarters.

When the system was up and running, it would show train consist information including loads and empties. Full waybill information was also included in the first report of a loaded car.

The heart of the MICS was a pair of computers electronically connected. One handled message switching, while the other was the MICS central computer. Both units were General Electric DataNet 30 computers with

It is 7:52 a.m. in the morning at Spring Garden, California and train 17 is 25 miles and 42 minutes out of Portola. On the other hand, Manifest Freight Symbol TOF, running as Extra 913A East is well ahead of schedule in this TCS territory meet in October, 1959. TOF was an Oakland to Roper Yard (Salt Lake City) train service. (Bob Larson)

three disc files, eight magnetic tape units, a high-speed printer and a card reader. As far as the Message Switching and Data Collection unit was concerned, the MICS computer was simply another station.

The next phase of the telecommunications was the development of a microwave system that at first extended from Sacramento to Portola, a distance of 180 miles by railroad. The company planned on completing the system from San Francisco to Portola by the end of 1970. (18)

Every once in awhile, something will go wrong. In this case a six car derailment in Stockton required the wrecker, and the 916A is heading up the "Work Extra" for this clean up job in July, 1958. Wrecker No. 37 is coupled to the GP7. (Bob Larson)

The computer systems were revamped throughout the 1970s to cover the increasing needs of car utilization and shipper service. After the merger with the Union Pacific and the Missouri Pacific, the MoPac's computer system was phased in throughout the entire system. In addition to the new computer systems that were placed in operation, there were a host of many other changes that took place with the WP for freight service improvements.

The company began a new marketing program during the late 1970s, which went beyond the usual sales or traffic department pitch. In this case, the company began a program to determine customer needs. The sales people became part of a marketing services unit, which in turn was supported by marketing research and development. (19)

At the same time, there was also a new separate intermodal department created. Evidence of the faith in the intermodal service came in several ways such as the then new Raygo Wagner lift-on / lift-off crane called a "Super Packer" that went into service at the Oakland Terminal in early 1979. (20)

The Marketing Development group was converted to a commodity based system in four categories:

> Bulk Freight of all types
> Metals
> Machinery
> All others including food, wine, paper
> and lumber

In fact during the late 1970s, the biggest single revenue contributor was food and various kindred products such as canned goods. This group accounted for more than 27% of the total gross revenues. The next largest group was transportation equipment with 14%. Contributing more than 5% each were primary metal products, lumber and wood products (except furniture); chemical and allied products; and finally pulp, paper and allied products. The three largest customers at that time were Ford Motor Company, the U.S. Government, and the United States Steel which accounted for a combined 22% of the 1978 revenues.

The marketing approach brought about many positive results. The year 1979 was one of the best ever for the canned goods shippers because of the coordinated car supply established, which obtained extra cars from connecting lines. Many of these cars came from railroads in the midwest through coordinated efforts of WP's transportation and marketing service groups in cooperation with contributing carriers.

Another aspect of the new marketing thrust was to attract new industry on the WP. One of the new industries was the CPC Corn Plant, which went into operation around 1981. Other examples included a J. C. Penney distribution center at Reno, a grain receiving facility near Modesto for Foster Farms, a Fearn International (a division of Kellogg's) food products plant at Milpitas, California, and two corrugated paper box plants, one an Owen-Illinois installation at Tracy, and the other a Container Corporation of America plant at Milpitas.

Still other projects included the development of a vehicle distribution ramp for autos and trucks at Oakland, including Chrysler and U.S. built Volkswagen Rabbits; and a tractor and agricultural implement ramp at Stockton. Both of these facilities served all of Northern California. These projects involved a total logistics system of services, pricing, properties and equipment, all coordinated by the WP into a synergistic system. All of the work was the result of the new marketing approach, which addressed shipper needs. (20)

When the WP merged with the Union Pacific, the average age of the motive power and car fleet was around 15 years old. The railroad was able to contribute a solid fleet of equipment to the new system. During the late 1980s and early 90s, Western Pacific equipment was coming out of the paint shops carrying WP reporting marks with the Union Pacific insignias. However, this era was short lived.

FREIGHT TRAIN NUMBERS & SYMBOLS

The Western Pacific freight trains throughout most of the company's history carried a variety of train numbers. Beginning in the 1960s, the company began designating the various freight trains with an alpha system. The following tables list the freight trains during various time periods from the 1940s until the Union Pacific merger.

Freight Train Numbers - 1940s		
Train Number	Origin	Destination
54	Oakland	Salt Lake City
62	Oakland	Salt Lake City
78	Stockton	Salt Lake City
61	Salt Lake City	Oakland
53	Salt Lake City	Oakland
77	Salt Lake City	Oakland
154	Keddie	Bieber
178	Keddie	Bieber
153	Bieber	Keddie
177	Bieber	Keddie
253	San Jose	Niles
254	Niles	San Jose
219	Reno	Portola
220	Portola	Reno

Source:

Western Pacific's Eastern Division Timetable No. 41, July 6, 1947.
Western Pacific's Western Division Timetable No. 35, July 6, 1947.

Freight Train Numbers - 1960s		
Symbol or Number	Origin	Destination
TOF	Oakland	Salt Lake City
EBM	Oakland	Salt Lake City
GGM	Oakland	Stockton
GGM/FB	Stockton	Salt Lake City
EXP	Stockton	Bieber
NCX	Stockton	Bieber (Portola)
SWG	Oakland (Stockton)	Bieber
SJP	San Jose	Stockton
ARF	Stockton	San Jose
PC	Salt Lake City	Oakland
CAL	Bieber (Portola)	Stockton
CFS	Salt Lake City	Oakland
PBF	Salt Lake City	Oakland
GWS	Bieber	Stockton
153	Bieber	Keddie
155	Bieber	Keddie
154	Keddie	Beiber
156	Keddie	Beiber
219	Reno	Portola
220	Portola	Reno

GP7 No. 711 has in tow just one steel bay window caboose as the sole consist of the Keddie to Portola shuttle train, which operated as Extra 711 East in the TCS territory. The cab hop has just now arrived at its destination. (1959, Bob Larson)

59

During the early 1970s, the WP operated three trains each way on the inside gateway with the following numbers:

7 (BN 137)	Bieber to Keddie	**Note**: All of these trains
11 (BN 171)		operated to and from
		Stockton.
9 (BN 139)		
8 (BN 138)	Keddie to Bieber	
4 (BN 140)		
10 (BN 170)		

Freight Train Symbols Operated Pre-Union Pacific 1970s through 1981.

Symbol	Train Name and Service Designation
OMW	Overland Mail West
GGV	Golden Gate Vans
B-PBF	Piggyback Forwarder
TOF	Trailers
COFC	Containers
XKI	
CCVX	
BAF	Bay Area Forwarder
OME	Overland Mail East
GGM	Golden Gate Manifest
WPX	Western Pacific Manifest
AWPX	Western Pacific Manifest
WPV	Western Pacific Vans
SJT	San Jose Turn
SWG	Santa Fe - Western Pacific - Great Northern (Burlington Northern)
GWS	See SWG
WMX	Westbound Mail
CIX	California - Illinois Express

Source: WP Freight Train Designations

One of the morning Stockton switch jobs, with Baldwin switcher No. 581 (Type VO-1000), is adding a caboose to the rear of symbol freight NCX. The NCX operated over the main line as an extra to Keddie, and then over the Fourth Sub to Bieber as train 156. (October 30, 1965, Author's Collection)

Switch engines in pick up and delivery service are as important as the main line freight, but not nearly as glamorous. The Afternoon Switch Job with the 605 for power has just finished spotting an empty gondola on Third Street in Oakland. The car will pick up a load before heading back east to its home road, the Lehigh Valley. (1967, Author's Collection)

The Western Pacific's freight traffic continued to grow for most of its existence as an individual railroad. In fact, the WP actually handled more freight in the early 1980s than it did in World War II. The following tables illustrate the growth in WP freight traffic, the marketing traffic mix prior to the merger, and the examples of the seasonal trends of freight traffic.

Annual Total Freight Tonnage	
Year	Tonnage
1912	1,000,000
1913	1,215,000
1914	1,199,000
1915	1,034,000
1916	1,452,000
1917	2,329,000
1918	2,689,000
1919	2,697,000
1920	2,699,000
1921	1,706,000
1922	2,120,000
1923	2,875,100
1924	3,078,000
1925	3,521,000
1926	3,709,000
1927	3,890,000
1928	3,977,000
1929	3,981,000
1930	3,775,000
1931	3,070,000
1932	2,670,000
1933	2,765,000
1934	3,211,000
1935	3,127,000
1936	3,733,000
1937	4,103,000
1938	3,675,000
1939	4,163,000
1940	4,617,000
1941	6,054,000
1942	8,561,000
1943	9,386,000
1944	9,527,000
1945	10,249,000
1946	8,856,000
1947	8,478,000
1948	7,767,000
1949	6,548,000
1950	7,308,000
1951	8.061,000
1952	7,559,000
1953	7,559,000
1954	6,560,000
1955	7,420,000
1956	7,647,000
1957	7,388,000
1958	6,910,000
1959	7,069,000
1960	7,160,000
1961	7,563,000
1962	7,791,000
1963	8,161,000
1964	8,300,000
1965	8,771,000
1966	8,925,000
1967	8,458,000
1968	9,283,000
1969	9,522,000
1970	9,292,000
1971	9,358,000
1972	9,741,000
1973	10,279,000
1974	10,460,000
1975	9,196,000
1976	9,061,000
1977	9,496,000
1978	10,003,000
1979	10,162,000
1980	10,454,000
1981	10,316,000

The year 1981 was the last full year of independent operation by the Western Pacific Railroad.

Sources: Annual Reports, Poor's Railroad Volumes, Moody's Railroad or Transportation Volumes from 1912 to 1981.

MARKETING MIX

During the last full year of independent operation in 1981, the Western Pacific carried the following marketing mix of freight shipments:

Farm Products	7.5%
Food and Kindred	25.3%
Lumber	4.9%
Pulp and Paper	7.1%
Chemicals	6.3%
Stone, Clay, etc.	3.2%
Metal Products	7.3%
Machinery	.4%
Transportation Equip.	3.1%
Freight Forwarding	.9%
Miscellaneous	4.3%
Total	**100.0%**

SEASONAL TRENDS

The following data shows the amount of percentage points of business per month during the ten year blocks of 1930 to 1939 and 1960 to 1969.

Month	1930s	1960s
Jan.	6.88	8.48
Feb.	5.88	7.43
Mar.	6.92	9.76
Apr.	7.24	7.55
May	8.04	8.16
June	7.76	7.55
July	8.37	7.64
Aug.	9.41	8.29
Sept.	10.51	8.86
Oct.	12.36	9.14
Nov.	8.86	8.40
Dec.	7.77	8.74
Averages:	**8.33**	**8.33**

During the later years, the WP had less swings in its month to month traffic patterns. It can also be said that the there is much to learn from the Western Pacific Railroad's marketing and operations approach for securing new traffic as well as retaining shippers for repeat business. It is an example of how a transportation company can develop a sense of community with and for its shippers, which brings about a strong base line for growth and development over decades. It has long run benefits.

The Wisconsin Central, which was a spin off from the Soo Line Railroad in the 1980s, is still another example of customer - company long term working relationships, which means a stronger base line for a profit. Perhaps one of the things that the larger railroads, i.e., mega-mergers could or should do is to create "brand" names for different types of services. One example might be "Western Pacific Intermodal Services." But that is a subject of another book. The important thing to remember is because of the Western Pacific's working relationship between the company and shippers, it built a successful long term freight traffic pattern.

61

Endnotes:

1. Railway Age, May 10, 1930, p. 1152.
2. Western Pacific Railroad Passenger Timetable, May 15, 1935
3 to 11 RAILWAY AGE with the following dates:
3. April 5, 1941, p. 615.
4. March 27, 1943, p. 610
5. Ibid.
6. Ibid.
7. May 15, 1948, p. 991.
8. January 7, 1952, p. 52.
9. Ibid.
10. February 18, 1950, p. 325.
11. March 30, 1953. p. 11.
12 and 13. Western Pacific Division Timetables, July 6, 1947, October 25, 1959 and April 24, 1960.
14 to 17 RAILWAY AGE
14. October 28, 1954, p. 8.
15. May 23, 1955, p. 4.
16. April 20, 1959, p. 10.
17. October 31, 1967, p. 100.
18. "On Western Pacific Computer Help Balance Car Supply-and-Demand," RAILWAY AGE, January 26, 1970, p. 22.
19. Frank Malone, "Western Pacific: A Key Piece in the Western Puzzle," RAILWAY AGE, November 12, 1979, p. 17.
20. Frank Malone, p. 19.

Work Extra 912A West is handling a gravel train at James, California while building the new line to accommodate the new Oroville Dam, which when built would flood the original main line. (Bob Larson)

This photo shows part of the new line at James, California on the Third Subdivision, 19.1 miles west of Oroville Yard. In this case, Extra 909A East is in the siding for a westbound train on the main line in Traffic Control System territory. (Bob Larson, August, 1963)

The long shadows of January 1, 1965 are nearly covering the GP35, the 3011 at Winnemuca, California. The new 3011 is the second such unit with that number, as the first had been involved in a derailment on the SP. That company replaced the unit with a new 3011.

The 3011 is heading up the B/PBF (Bay Piggyback Freight), which is running as Extra 3011 West in TCS Territory on the First Subdivision of the Eastern Division. (Bob Larson)

The time is 11:45 a.m. on May 30, 1967, and manifest freight symbol CFS is awaiting the hi ball to depart Oroville Yard for Stockton. It will operate as Extra 922A West over the 113.1 mile Second Subdivision in about 3 hours, 15 minutes. (Author's Collection)

The WP restructured the subdivisions in 1965 with a renumbering of the Eastern Subdivisions. For example, the First Sub between Winnemucca and Portola became the new Fifth Subdivision. The scene in this photo is Scotts, California, which is 24.3 miles east of Portola. In this superb winter scene, Extra 923A West has hit the east remote control switch of Scotts in TCS Territory, and is continuing on toward Portola and ultimately an Oakland Yard destination. The reader will notice in this February, 1967 photo, the F units appear to still be in command, but this would soon change. (Bob Larson)

This 1967 view of Symbol Freight B/PBF shows the first run of the new U30Bs. Running as Extra 752 West, the train is waiting for an eastbound manifest at Del Rio, 143.6 miles from Stockton with a 122 car siding in TCS Territory. Symbol B/PBF is en route from Salt Lake City to Oakland. (Bob Larson)

A very important train on the Western Pacific was the APF, which operated westward from Stockton to Niles Junction, and then eastward over the San Jose Branch to San Jose Yard. The train performed a crucial service for the Ford Distribution center at Milpitas. Indeed, the APF, running as Extra 726 East on the branch, is engaged in switching bi-level and tri-level flats and auto parts equipment for the facility in this photo, taken on a Sunday afternoon, March 30, 1969. (Author's Collection)

Three F units and Spreader No. 7 arrive at Bieber after clearing the Fourth Subdivision of snow over the entire 111.8 mile line. According to Bob Larson, they had been out on the line for five days snow plowing, which is often very frustrating work. The clouds in the background seem to indicate that more snow is on the way in this February, 1970 scene. Bieber Yard was governed by Great Northern Railway timetable and operating rules, and the Burlington Northern merger was still a month away when this photo was taken. (Bob Larson)

Swinging back to the Fourth Subdivision for awhile, it is June, 1972, and traffic is a bit heavy for the moment at Almanor, 25.7 miles east of Keddie (railroad direction) on the line to Bieber. Extra 2252 East, the Westwood Turn, is in the siding and is being passed by train 154, en route from Keddie to Bieber and a Burlington Northern (ex-Great Northern) connection. (Bob Larson)

One of the things that can make railroads so attractive as a hobby, and as a transportation concept to study, is its ability to change to accommodate shipper needs. Sometimes these changes can be reflected in day-to-day operations. This photo was taken in June, 1972, of the same trains as shown in the previous photo but on a different day. The Westwood Turn is powered by four F units and train 154 is headed up by a Burlington Northern F45, No. 6632. As far as the dispatcher is concerned, Extra 913A East is being passed by train 154, a Second Class schedule in the division timetable. The Bieber line was not equipped with a Traffic Control System. (Bob Larson)

(Left) Although some F units were still doing the snow jobs and other work details, the task of moving the main line freights fell virtually completely to the heavy duty GP35s and GP40s. It is September 1, 1970, and GP40 No. 3522 is leading three other units on a drag west, identified to the dispatcher as Extra 3522 West. The train is ready to depart Portola, and the reader will note the green units with the silver and orange GP35 holding out for good measure. Things were changing on the Western Pacific, and the company was just about to enter the last decade of independent operation. (Bob Larson)

By now the reader maybe wondering what is the Westwood Turn? The Westwood Turn was a local assignment out of Keddie that operated from Keddie to Westwood and Return. Hence the term, Westwood Turn. The train departed Keddie and worked at Crescent Mills, Greenville, Almanor (where this photo of Extra 2257 East was taken), Clear Creek Junction, and finally Westwood. (Bob Larson)

With a mixture of WP and BN power, symbol freight No. 138, running as train 8, arrives at Keddie, California with a through train for the Burlington Northern. (Bob Larson, June, 1972)

As a prelude of things to come in the 1980s, symbol freight GGV, running as Extra 3545 West at Flanigan, Nevada; not only displays the WP's last paint scheme, but also the inclusion of Union Pacific power. The GGV has just completed a meet with an eastbound, which is barely visible to the right of the photo - TCS Territory. (Bob Larson, October 26, 1979)

Extra 3001 West has a long string of covered hopper cars at Red Rock, California, on the Fifth Subdivision. (The Eastern and Western Divisions were combined.) It is October 4, 1981, and within a short time span, the Western Pacific will become part of the Feather River Division of the Union Pacific. (Bob Larson)

We are now into July, 1983, and the local has tied up at North Reno Parr Yard. Western Pacific proudly stands out on the caboose and motive power, and really, it says it all! People really did know who the WP was. (Bob Larson)

We are now into the Union Pacific merger, and the mixtures are showing up. Sacramento Northern No. 711 sits with a Union Pacific caboose at Portola, California with the B&L local, the train that served the Loyalton Branch. (Bob Larson, April, 1984)

The Ruby Mountains serve as a back drop for Extra 2253 West running with three units and new automobiles just east of Elko, Nevada on Southern Pacific trackage - in the joint track territory. (John Ryczkowski)

The 3528 leads a mixed drag over paired WP-SP trackage east of Winnemuca. (John Ryczkowski)

Two extremely important junctions are at the ends of the WP-SP paired track territory. A westbound all-piggyback train comes off the SP rails at Weso, and back on to the WP trackage for the remainder of the trip to Oakland. Note the "END TCS" sign to the right of the WP rails, meaning End Traffic Control System in use on the WP. (John Ryczkowski)

Chapter 8

CAR FERRY SERVICES

This brief chapter takes a quick look at the Western Pacific's car ferry operations between Oakland and San Francisco. The service permitted the movement of freight car traffic beyond Oakland to the San Francisco area for pick up and delivery service for a wide number of customers. The WP also interchanged freight traffic with the Southern Pacific for pick up and delivery services within a short range in the San Francisco area.

Otherwise, freight traffic could be interchanged with the SP at San Jose. An entire book could be written on the car ferry operations. The following two photos illustrate part of the work by the WP's operation.

This photograph is valuable for two reasons. First of all, it illustrates the 25th Street boat slip for the WP car ferries. Secondly we have a rare photo of a wooden composite gondola, WP 4460, in service at the slip in June, 1947. The photo itself was taken from the front of a locomotive, with the four reacher flats strung out ahead of the motive power. Why the reacher or idler flats? The apron for loading and unloading freight cars was not designed for the weight of a locomotive. Although it may not be visible in the photo, there are grab irons across the front of the first idler car, just as one would have found on a switch engine during the mid-1940s. (Bob Larson Collection)

It is a foggy day - so what else is new at ocean sides throughout the world? Nevertheless, it is not so bad that Bob Larson cannot photograph the "Las Plumas," the last of the WP's car ferry services. The reader will note the "feather" and the "Western Pacific" name on the side of the ferry. It went without saying that the "Feather River" and the name "Western Pacific" were virtually synonymous. (Bob Larson, San Francisco, 1958)

Chapter 9

FREIGHT EQUIPMENT

This volume on the Western Pacific takes still another look at some of the WP freight equipment. It is primarily a pictorial survey of the variety of equipment along with the various number series for each group. The chapter is divided into the following categories:

> Box Cars
> Refrigerator Cars
> Hopper Cars
> Covered Hoppers
> Flat Cars
> Gondolas
> Cabooses

One of the items pointed out are some of the different paint and lettering schemes. This created quite a variety of the various periods of time right through to the Union Pacific merger. For photos of WP equipment in the various UP schemes, refer to the Epilogue.

We trust that this section will provide some additional information for modelers and the art of model railroading. When one stops to think about it, model railroading is a full conglomerate of art work ranging from painting, sculpturing (scenery construction), lettering, the design of various the layouts, as well as the detail work for the main lines, yards, and buildings of all types. And the art work doesn't stop there when one considers scratch building or kit bashing different models of motive power and rolling stock. Finally, modeling the Western Pacific equipment and trains keeps the railroad alive in our hearts since it has been folded completely into the Union Pacific System.

For roster references and other information regarding the Western Pacific freight car fleet, as well as the passenger and work car fleet, the reader may wish to refer to the Book: WESTERN PACIFIC LOCOMOTIVES AND CARS, written by this author and published by TLC in 1998.

Box Car No. 3019 (3011 - 3050) is a special type car with an 8 foot door, Damage Free equipment and a cushion underframe. The car was painted orange with a silver feather and black lettering. (Council Bluffs, November 26, 1955, Lou Schmitz)

Former Fruit Growers Express car 92266 (92264-92288) was acquired by the Western Pacific. (Omaha, December 28, 1980, Lou Schmitz)

Car 19399 (19301-19450) is a 50 foot car with a 15 foot double door. Painted in the box car red scheme, the group was built in 1953. (Dallas, Texas, 1961, Jay Williams Collection, Big Four Graphics)

WP 19530 (19501-19542) was built in 1951. The 40 foot car has a 50 ton capacity, and in this case was compartmentizer equipped. The car was painted in the aluminum colors with the "Rides Like a Feather" logo. (Jay Williams Collection, Big Four Graphics)

Car 20397 (20201-20550) was built in 1945. The car was painted in the box car red scheme, or otherwise known as the Oxide Red colors. The 40 foot car has a 6 foot door with a 50 ton capacity. (Collection of Jay Williams, Big Four Graphics)

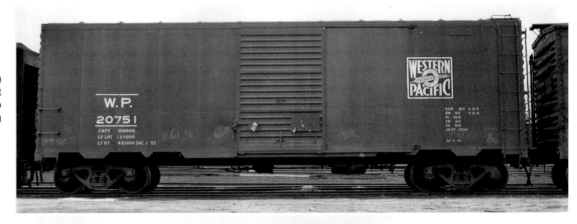

Box car 20751 (20551-20800) was built in 1947. The 40 foot car was rebuilt at Sacramento in 1955. (Jay Williams, Big Four Graphics)

40 foot Car 21068 (20821-21400) was equipped with a 7 foot door, and built in 1951. (Jay Williams, Big Four Graphics)

Car 38155 (38001-38225) was over 55 feet long with a 77 ton capacity and a 16 foot double door. Note the latest Feather Insignia. (Fremont, Nebraska, October 25, 1981, Lou Schmitz)

Car 38228 (38226-38325) was nearly identical to 38001 group complete with the 16 foot door. However, the car's capacity was actually 1000 pounds more than the earlier group. (Council Bluffs, Iowa, Feb. 20, 1984, Lou Schmitz)

Car 38260 illustrates the B end of the 38226-38325 group. (Council Bluffs, August 2, 1981, Lou Schmitz)

Car 38272 was painted with bright red doors. (Yermo, California, Feb. 21, 1994, Gordon Lloyd, Collection of Lou Schmitz)

WP 56161 (56101-56175) was an insulated box car with a single plug door. (Dallas, Texas, 1962, Collection of Jay Williams, Big Four Graphics)

Car 60418 (60411-60440) was a 58 foot insulated box car with a 9 foot plug door. (Council Bluffs, Iowa, June 29, 1980, Lou Schmitz)

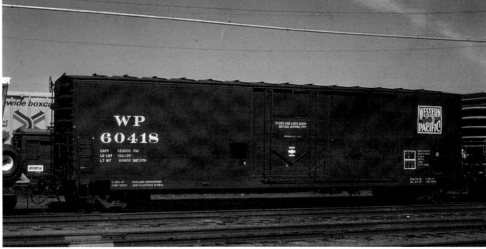

60771 (60651-60800) was a 58 foot insulated box car with a 15 foot plug door. (Omaha, December 23, 1984, Lou Schmitz)

Insulated box 62076 (62001-62225), 58 foot car with a 15 foot plug door. (Council Bluffs, May 19, 1985, Lou Schmitz)

Car 64029 (64001-64074) is another example of a 58 foot insulated box car with a 15 foot plug door. ((Fremont, Nebraska, October 25, 1981, Lou Schmitz)

Insulated box car 68722 (Council Bluffs, October, 1982, Lou Schmitz)

Pacific Fruit Express car 55327 was a classic wooden car lettered for the Western Pacific. PFE was a joint venture with the Union Pacific and Southern Pacific. (Council Bluffs, November 5, 1955, Lou Schmitz)

WP hopper car 10111 (10086-10200) was a 100 ton capacity car, 42 feet long. Photographed in iron ore service at Itasca, Wisconsin, C&NW, March, 1989, Thomas A. Dorin

Hopper car 10222 (10201-10230), 44 feet long with a 100 ton capacity. (Topeka, Kansas, June 2000, Larry Tiffany, Lou Schmitz Collection)

Car 10266 (10231-10295), a 44 foot car with 100 ton capacity. (Council Bluffs, June 21, 1987, Lou Schmitz)

Car 10553 (10301-10575) , 39 foot car with 100 ton capacity. Photographed in stone service at Superior, Wisconsin. (Thomas A. Dorin)

Car 10798 (10701-10800), 35 feet long, in ballast service. (Salt Lake City, June 21, 1996, Lou Schmitz)

Hopper 10848 (10800-11000), a 42 foot car with 100 ton capacity. (Council Bluffs, June 21, 1987, Lou Schmitz)

WP hopper car 10929 (Salt Lake City, June 21, 1996, Lou Schmitz)

Hopper car 70071 (70000-70240) was part of a group purchased for coal service. The 53 foot cars had a 100 ton capacity, and were often seen in the Superior, Wisconsin area. (Council Bluffs, October 13, 1979, Lou Schmitz)

(Right and Below) Two examples of the 100 ton grain hoppers include the 12021 (12001-12050) and the 12073 (12051-12100). 12021 photographed at Council Bluffs in January, 1981, while the 12073's portrait was taken at Grand Island, Nebraska on June 2, 1985. (Lou Schmitz)

Car 2151 was from the 2151 to 2159 group, which were 64 feet long. (Council Bluffs, September 10, 1978, Lou Schmitz)

77

Bulkhead flat car No. 1451 (1451-1490) was 70 feet long with a 93 ton capacity. (Council Bluffs, August 21, 1983, Lou Schmitz)

Bulkhead 1455 illustrated with a load of lumber. (Grand Island, Nebraska, July 14, 1985, Lou Schmitz)

Covered Auto Rack cars TTGX 910502 with WP markings. (Omaha, June 4, 1989, Lou Schmitz)

Auto Rack car CTTX 852688 was an open top car. (Omaha, March 11, 1984, Lou Schmitz)

Mill gondola 9065 (9051-9065) was a 70 foot car designed to handle hot steel billets. (Enid, Oklahoma, September 20, 1983. Marshall Higgins, Lou Schmitz Collection)

Mill gondola 6650 (6601-6800) were 57 foot gons with an 80 ton capacity. (Council Bluffs, Iowa, May 6, 1989, Lou Schmitz)

(Above and Below) The short 34 foot solid bottom gondolas were originally built for the Oro Dam Service. The 6203 and 6207 were part of the 6201 to 6210 group with a 100 ton capacity. In many ways, the cars resemble some of the solid bottom ore cars built for the Reserve Mining Company Railroad in Minnesota and the Southern Pacific ore cars. (Lou Schmitz, 6207 in 1999, 6203 in 1988)

What better way to end the mini-chapter on freight equipment than a look at three bay window cabooses with three different lettering schemes:

435 at Council Bluffs in August, 1985
450 at Council Bluffs in February, 1982
478 at Council Bluffs in May, 1974

All three photos by Lou Schmitz

Chapter 10

MOTIVE POWER PICTORIAL REVIEW

The purpose of this chapter is to provide a pictorial review of the Western Pacific's motive power history until the Union Pacific merger. The photos illustrate the various types of power with their respective number series and other information. The first section covers the steam locomotive roster with different views, while the second part illustrates additional diesel motive power.

This pictorial review of WP Steam coincides with the roster listed on page 7 of the *Western Pacific Locomotives and Cars* (published by TLC Publishing, 1998). All photos are from the TLC Publishing Collection unless otherwise designated.

Steam Power

No. 11 was part of the first group of steam power purchased by the Western Pacific in 1906 from Baldwin. No. 11 was part of the 1 to 20 series, Road Class 1, Symbol C-43.

No. 30 purchased in 1909 from Alco and part of series 21 to 65, Road Class 21, Symbol C-43. Left side view.

2-8-0 No. 47 illustrates the right side of the Road Class 21 group.

2-8-0 No. 62 had its portrait taken between assignments at Stockton on June 19, 1938 - and it is ready to go for an extra train with white flags flying on the boiler. The 62 was scrapped in February of 1950.

Ten-wheeler No. 73 was part of the second group of steam power ordered by the WP. The 73 was built by Alco in 1908, part of series 71 to 85, Class 71, Symbol TP-29.

No. 79 heads up a passenger train at Oakland on September 4, 1933. The engine illustrates the fine care that the WP provided its motive power and equipment.

The WP purchased a second group of Ten-Wheelers from Alco in 1909, Class 86, Symbol TP-29, number series 86 to 106. No. 86 was photographed in service at Stockton in July, 1938. This piece of motive power was scrapped in December, 1949.

Ten-Wheeler No. 99 was heading up an extra freight train in this photo, location unknown. Note the white flags on the front of the boiler. Note the differences of both left sides of the 86 and the 99.

No. 106 illustrates the right side of the 86 to 106 group, and is in action on the head-end of a passenger train. Location unknown.

One of the WP's second hand pieces of motive power was the 122. This Ten-Wheeler and its sister 121 were built by Richmond in 1896. The WP classified the two locomotives as 121, Symbol TF-17.

No. 157 illustrates the right side of the Class 151 group.

The Western Pacific purchased a group of superb and handsome 4-8-2s from the Florida East Coast in 1936. Number 171 was part of series 171 to 180, Class 171, Symbol MTP-44. The 171 is between assignments in this photo at Oakland on January 3, 1937.

The 4-8-2 No. 173 was photographed at Stockton in May, 1952. It was the last of the 4-8-2 group to be scrapped. The ex-Florida East Coast power did a magnificent job for the Western Pacific.

The Western Pacific, like virtually all of the western railroads in North America, also invested in the articulated Mallet type of steam motive power. No. 201 is a 2-6-6-2, part of the 201-205 series, Class 201, Symbol M-80, built by Alco in 1917. The 201 is shown here at Keddie, California in May, 1938. The last month of operation for the 201 was in May, 1951, and it went to the scrap yard in May, 1952. So it sat around for a year doing nothing, except perhaps being a subject of badly needed photography of steam power.

The next group of mallets, 2-6-6-2s, were the series 206 to 210, Class 206, Symbol M-80, built by Alco in 1924. The 208 was photographed at Stockton in June, 1952. It was the last of this group of Mallets, and was scrapped in January, 1953.

The next group of Mallets, 2-8-8-2s, came in 1931 from Baldwin. No. 251 was the first of the 251 to 256 series, Class 251, Symbol M-137-151. The 251 is shown here at Oakland in 1952 with a rather forlorn look. It has lost its insignia, and will soon be on the way to the scrap heap.

No. 254 is in action and ready to handle a time freight. This view shows the right side of these magnificent locomotives. Date and location unknown.

Number 260, the last of the group, is all steamed up and ready to go. What an incredible sight with a meticulous sound that would have given Mozart and many other composers new ideas to write music about.

The first Mikados arrived in 1918 from Alco. Number 303 is part of the 301 to 305 group, Class 301, Symbol MK-60. The 303 was photographed at Stockton in June, 1952, and was scrapped in January, 1953. It could brag about 34 years of service for the Western Pacific freight shippers. It played a significant role for the American economy.

Number 306 launched the second group of 2-8-2s from 1919. However, they were not originally built for the Western Pacific. The group 306 to 310 was purchased from the Elgin, Joliet and Eastern Railway, originally numbered 802 to 806. The second group was Class 306, Symbol MK-60.

No. 329 was part of the 327 to 331 series, Class 327. The portrait of 329 was taken at Stockton in 1952, still in service. No. 329 was eventually scrapped in December, 1953.

The next group of Mallets came from Alco in 1938. Numbered from 401 to 407, the 4-6-6-4s were part of the class 401, Symbol MK-100. This left side view of the 401 was taken in 1952 and it has lost its insignia for its routing to the scrap yard, which took place in June, 1952. Its last photo was taken in Oakland.

Right side view of the 402., which was taken in 1952. The engine was scrapped in June, 1952. Number 402 had the distinction and honor of being exhibited at the Chicago Railroad Fair in 1949. The railroad industry should do another such fair as we move into the 21st Century. After all, it is only railroad technology that can solve the transportation problems through a coordinated effort with other modes of transport.

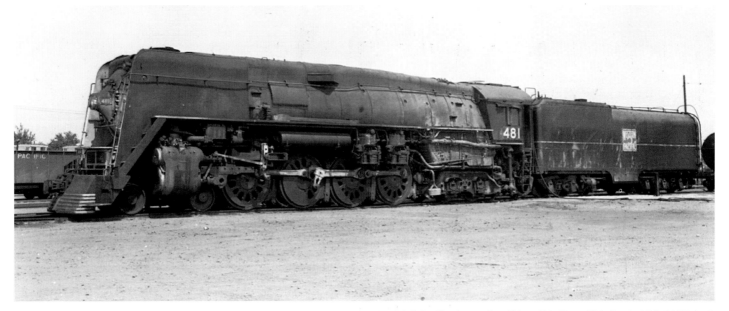

The last steam power to be a part of the Western Pacific roster were the streamlined 4-8-4s, Number series 481 to 486, Class 481, Symbol GS-64-77, built in 1943 as part of a Southern Pacific order. The 481 was photographed at Stockton in 1952, and it was sold to the SP in 1953 for parts.

Right side view of the 482.

The Streamlined 4-8-4s had one of the shortest life spans on the WP, with dieselization and all of that good stuff. The 486 was last operated by the railroad in January, 1953.

No. 166 illustrates the left side of the Class 163. Photographed at Stockton, California in July, 1952. This engine was purchased from a copper mining company and its original number was 88. It was purchased by the WP in 1927.

The second group of 2-8-8-2s, number series 257 to 260, Class 257, Symbol M-137-151, were built by Baldwin in 1938. The 259 has lost its insignia as it is 1952 and it too is on the way to the scrap heap. Compared to some motive power, the Mallets had a relatively short life span from 1938 to 1952.

Left side view of the 402.

Portrait of the 172, location and date unknown.

Left side view of the 404, which is at the very end of its career in 1952 at Stockton. The engine was scrapped that year.

No. 124 was indeed a rare piece of power and the only one of its kind on the WP. This 2-8-0 was built by Baldwin in 1882, Class 124, Symbol C-23. Note the style of headlight. Location and date of photo unknown.

No. 164 was part of the second group of 0-6-0s, number series 163 to 166, purchased from Alco in 1915 and also 1919. The WP classified the group as 163, with the symbol S-34.

DIESEL SECTION

The Western Pacific diesel locomotive fleet history spread over a period of nearly five decades from 1939 through the Union Pacific merger. In order to service the motive power, the WP set up fueling and service facilities from San Jose to Salt Lake City's Roper Yard. Here is a listing of those stations with such facilities:

San Jose
Oakland
Stockton including a Special Shop for Servicing
South Sacramento
Oroville
Keddie
Portola
Elko
Roper Yard at Salt Lake City

Let's take a quick look at the Stockton diesel shop which was established in the early 1940s.

One of the philosophies of the Western Pacific was the creation of a top quality maintenance program for both track and equipment. A very sound idea because it creates long run benefits, which are actually less expensive. Top maintenance of the tracks is far less expensive than a series of derailments because of poor maintenance. Extending the life of motive power works in the same way.

Stockton was one of the busiest yards, and was the railroad's largest freight terminal yard. The WP created an addition to the existing roundhouse especially designed to handle the diesel motive power, especially the switch engines assigned to the terminal. In the mid-1940s, the WP had assigned five Baldwin switchers to Stockton.

The new additional end stall was designed specifically for the switch engines. It was designed to provide rapid servicing and maintenance. It was very similar to other WP terminals where switch engines, and road power were handled. What did it look like?

A wooden wall separated the diesel section from the steam engine stalls. This was done to prevent the steam power soot to contaminate the exposed diesel engine parts during repairs and servicing. One end of the diesel stall was arranged for inspection and servicing while the other part handle various types of repairs.

The inspection section contained both upper and lower platforms. Such an arrangement permitted ready and safe access to the running boards and diesel engine parts. Part of the upper platform could be folded back to provide appropriate clearance when a diesel unit was moved into the stall. A well lighted pit below the track level permitted ready inspection of the traction motors and running gear. A sloping floor with drainage gutters on both sides carried off accumulations of oil and water. A jib crane was also part of the facility which permitted easy removal of cylinder heads.

The diesel workshop was a "lean-to" type of building extended beyond the orginal roundhouse outer wall and measured 30 X 20 feet, and was connected to one end of the stall. The area was equipped with work benches as well as lockers for all types of hand and portable tools required for locomotive maintenance. A fuel injection pump and fuel injection nozzle test sets were used as well as a gauge tester for calibrating gauge pressures on the locomotives.

The engine hour stall was 120 feet long with a 72 foot reinforced concrete engine pit including rustic walls, concrete foundations and the lean to workshop. Part of the equipment included a 20 foot, 1 ton jib crane, a 20,000 gallon steel diesel oil storage tank complete with pump and fittings as well as electrical connections.

Source: The Baldwin, Vol. 4, Number 3, First and Second Quarter, 1948. Published by the Baldwin Locomotive Works, Philadelphia, Pennsylvania.

Following is a pictorial of part of the Western Pacific diesel motive power fleet. For a complete pictorial review, the reader may wish to refer to the first volume of this work: WESTERN PACIFIC LOCOMOTIVES AND CARS, pages 30 to 55.

The WP diesel motive power fleet ranged from the early switch engine models from Electro-Motive, Alco and Baldwin to the Covered Wagon units for freight and passenger service; and finally the GP35s, 40s, and 40-2s from EMD; and U Boats from General Electric. Following is a brief pictorial review of the WP diesel power.

In the background the Stockton roundhouse can be observed in part behind the WP F units 919D and 918B plus a B unit. The F7As are between assignments at Stockton on September 9, 1966. (Author's Collection)

The 901A was the first FT unit on the Western Pacific. The FT number series extended from 901A-D to 912A, D. The B units were numbered 901B, C to 912B, C. All of the FT units were retired by 1966. (Portola, Bob Larson)

FT No. 908D was equipped with a snow plow on the pilot. The reader may recall the photo of the steamer with the same type of plow. The 908D with its sister B unit to the rear was photographed in 1964. (Bob's Photos)

The 914D was part of the group of F7A's, number series 913A-D to 924A-D purchased in 1950 and 51. The B units were numbered 913B-C to 924B-C. No. 914D, with a second unit, are at Stockton on a Sunny December 23 in 1967. (Author's Collection)

No. 920A leads a three unit consist between runs at Stockton. The 920 is displaying the full orange paint scheme with the black lettering. (Bob Larson)

We have to take a look at the last of the number series of the F7s, the gracious and colorful 924A. Again we have a photo of a layover at Stockton on an April morning in 1967. (Author's Collection)

No. 919A in the orange scheme illustrating the placement of the words "Radio Equipped" below the cab window. With the solid orange scheme, the top black stripe was painted all the to the entry door. One other point, the number of units were placed at the bottom next to the rear of the orange motive power. Note the location of the 919A at the lower left in this photo. (Sacramento, 1967, Jay Williams Collection, Big Four Graphics)

The F7s were also equipped with the snow plows on the pilots. No. 920D heads up a six unit consist at Stockton in 1971. The second unit in the consist is a U30B, No. 756 from the 751-769 group, which were later renumbered to 3051 to 3071. The third and four units are from the former Spokane, Portland and Seattle Railway. This would mean the power has been and will be working on a train for the Fourth Subdivision to Bieber, and a connection with the Burlington Northern. This was an interesting example of pooling power for through train operations. (Bob's Photos)

A bit of a top view of a five unit combination coming off the Keddie Wye bridge with F units doing most of the honors. The Geep fits nicely into the consist. What a view for train watching. (Bob's Photos)

The 805A was a FP7 and part of the 804A. D - 805A, D series. The FP7s and their B unit companions, were assigned to the California Zephyr, trains 17 and 18 between Salt Lake City and Oakland. They were equipped with steam generators. They was also a group of F7 As and Bs, number series 801A to 803A plus the 801D, which was purchased from the New York, Ontario and Western. The F3B units, such as behind the 805A were numbered from 801B, C to 803B, C. The F7Bs were numbered 804B to 806B. Note the wings as part of the Western Pacific insignia for the passenger units. (1967, Bob's Photos)

GP7 No. 705 (Series 701 to 713) were built in 1952 and 53. The WP units were a bit unique with the different type of headlights. GP7s 711 and 712 were sold to the Sacramento Northern Railway in 1971. The 705 is shown here at the locomotive terminal at Stockton on October 30, 1965. (Author's Collection)

The next phase of the famous Electro-Motive Division Geeps were the GP9s. No. 731 was part of the 725 to 732 series, built in 1955. The 731 was in service when its portrait was taken at Oakland in March, 1972. (Mac Owen Collection)

The Western Pacific purchased two sets of power from General Electric. The U30Bs, such as the 3061, arrived on the WP in 1967 and 69. Originally numbered 751 to 769, the U30s were renumbered to 3051 to 3071 in 1971. The 3061 is shown here at Oakland in October, 1976.

The WP's other General Electrics were 15 U23Bs, 2251 to 2265, purchased in 1972.
(TLC Collection)

The WP invested in the second generation power, such as GP35 No. 3004 (3001 to 3022) in 1963 and 65. The units operated system wide in all types of freight services. (Jay Williams Collection, Big Four Graphics)

GP40 No. 3523 was part of the 3501 to 3544 series purchased in 1966 and 1971. The 3523 was photographed on the Milwaukee Road in St. Paul in 1987. (Patrick C. Dorin)

Now here is an interesting twist for GP40 No. 3526. It is MU'd with a Milwaukee Road unit at the former Northern Pacific yard in Duluth, Minnesota. The pair are laying over between runs of the overnight time freight on the Milwaukee Road between the St. Paul Yard and Duluth. The Rices Point Terminal (Duluth) was still used for making up time freights and grain trains in the 1980s. The Yard still functions for grain and other industrial switching services as this is being written in mid-2003. (Patrick C. Dorin)

Epilogue

THE UNION PACIFIC SYSTEM

The Western Pacific became part of the Union Pacific Railroad System in December, 1982. For a short while, Western Pacific motive power was to be painted in the UP scheme with Western Pacific lettering. However, after but one single unit was painted as such, the policy gave way to motive power simply being repainted with Union Pacific lettering. On the other hand, freight car equipment was up through 1989 being repainted with WP reporting marks and UP insignias.

The WP routing provides a direct and through route to and from the east, such as St. Louis and other points south as well as to Chicago and the Twin Cities. With the merger with the Missouri Pacific, and the subsequent mergers with the Southern Pacific, and the Chicago and North Western, the UP serves virtually all of the territory west, northwest, and south of Chicago to Texas, the Southwest and the entire Pacific Coast.

Backtracking a bit, when the UP/MP/WP came together, a system of 22,000 miles with over 3000 locomotives and 130,000 freight cars was created. This in turn created a potential for improved service. Specifically, the WP's main line was again upgraded, which actually was a WP standard for decades. Expedited trains were soon placed on a 22 hour, 30 minute schedule between Salt Lake City and Oakland. North Platte/Oakland trains were placed in service, such as the NPST (North Platte - Stockton) and NPOAZ, which is a North Platte - Oakland Intermodal train was well as their eastbound counterparts.

The Western Pacific had had an ongoing track program. Although in the 1970s, that had been slowed down somewhat, the UP began a new program for the new Feather River Division. The first major plan involved the relaying of 316 miles of tangent main line and 75 miles of curves with new rail, and relay another 75 miles of track with second-hand rail, plus the insertion of over 500,000 ties, surfacing and lining of 949 miles of track and the upgrading of secondary and subsidiary lines with 103 miles of relay rail, 125,000 new ties, and surfacing/lining of 250 miles.

The poor subgrade conditions on the main line between Wendover and Garfield, Utah were to be corrected. This is the track that runs across the Utah Salt Flats, and much of it had been slow ordered to 40 miles per hour. The plan was to drive in stabilization pilings, provide between drainage, install sand fences on top of dikes, and the sledding of portions of this stretch of track. With the upgrading, the track speed was upgraded to 70 miles per hour for freight. (1)

The terminals at Salt Lake City were shifted from the D&GRW's Roper Yard to the UP's North Yard that eliminated the cross-town interchange and switching at both yards. (2)

Moving through the 1980s, the former Western Pacific was fully integrated into the UP System. Train traffic was as heavy or even heavier than the 1960s. The following table lists the through trains on the main line between Salt Lake City and Oakland during that period of time. (3)

Symbol	Origin	Destination	
STMI	Stockton	Milpitas	
NPST	North Platte	Stockton	
NPOAZ	North Platte	Oakland	Intermodal
APOA5X	Chicago	Oakland	Intermodal
APOA2X	Chicago	Oakland	Intermodal
APOA4X	Chicago	Oakland	Intermodal
SLOAZ	St. Louis	Oakland	Intermodal
SCST	Salt Lake City	Stockton	
OAAP2	Oakland	Chicago	Intermodal
OACSZ	Oakland	Chicago	Intermodal
OANPZ	Oakland	North Platte	Intermodal
MINPZ	Milpitas	North Platte	
NPMIZ	North Platte	Milpitas	Intermodal
OAAP6	Oakland	Chicago	Intermodal
OANP	Oakland	North Platte	
STSC	Stockton	Salt Lake City	

The schedules and operating days and times of the above list varied as the months and years rolled by. The Feather River Division, as the former WP main line was designated, was truly a "High Speed Railroad" for the freight services.

The Union Pacific eventually merged with the Southern Pacific, and whole new era of train services began. That is a subject of still another story about the Western Pacific trackage as well as the Southern Pacific lines and the UP System as a whole.

As a final note: During the 1990s, the WP trackage was part of the Los Angeles Service Unit. The name "Division" had been dropped from the nomenclature. The former WP main lines were divided into the following subdivisons:

> The Elko Subdivision from Smelter (Salt Lake City) to Portola
>
> The Canyon Subdivision from Portola to Oakland
>
> The Bieber Subdivision from Keddie to Bieber
>
> **Other lines included:**
>
> The Reno Branch
>
> San Jose Branch from Niles Junction to Milpitas
>
> The Tidewater Southern Subdivision from Stockton to Turlock

The merger with the Southern Pacific brought still other changes in the Service Units throughout the entire Union Pacific System. And finally, there is one more final note about activities on the former Western Pacific Railroad trackage. Part of the WP is now the route of a new commuter train service between Stockton and San Jose, California, the Altamont Commuter Express. As this is being written, three trains a day each way travel over the line (Refer to Chapter 6). One never knows what the future will bring.

> **Epilogue Endnotes:**
>
> 1. Gus Welty, "UP/MP/WP: A Whole Greater Than the Sum of the Parts," RAILWAY AGE, April 27, 1981, p. 20.
> 2. Ibid.
> 3. Symbol Freight Designations: Union Pacific Railroad Company

The 3532 headed up a passenger special on the WP with three UP coaches. The imagination can only wander to think of Western Pacific passenger equipment, such as business cars, etc., painted in the UP colors with Western Pacific lettering. If that had been the case, the WP would have joined the C&NW, SP, MP, Milwaukee Road, Wabash, Norfolk and Western, and the Pennsylvania Railroads with UP color scheme equipment. (Bob Larson)

What was once the most modern of the modern rolls over the former Feather River Division, such as SD60M, No. 6183 handling a west bound grain train on August 18, 1989 at Winnemuca, Nevada. (Bob Larson)

A wide variety of General Electric and Electro-Motive Division power team up to take Extra 2430 West over the Western Pacific trackage out of Salt Lake City in August, 1988. (Thomas A. Dorin)

No sooner had Extra 2430 West departed the UP Yard when Extra 3706 West departed the yard, while still another set of UP motive power switched back and forth to go to the engine facilities to the right of the photo - at Salt Lake City. (Thomas A. Dorin)

As we complete this section of photographs on Western Pacific trackage in the UP System, we turn our attention to "two" different kinds of trains not normally part of the WP atmosphere during the 1960s. In the first case a west bound intermodal train, Symbol OMW and running as Extra 6929 West displaying all of the characteristics of the modern day transportation services. (Bob Larson, 1984)

Western Pacific cabooses and motive power have ranged far and wide throughout the western and mid-western United States. UP's 2423 and caboose No. 483 were not uncommon sights at the Chicago and North Western's Itasca Yard in Superior, Wisconsin. Indeed, UP and MP motive power and MP cabooses were also frequently observed in Superior operating on all-rail ore trains from the Minnesota Mesabi Range to Utah. A real long haul! (Thomas A. Dorin)

Did Western Pacific freight disappear from the scene with the UP merger? WP equipment began showing up in the 1980s with WP reporting marks and UP insignias, such as WP Insulated Box Car No. 65434. (Lou Schmitz, Council Bluffs, Iowa, January 26, 1986)

WP Insulated Box Car No. 65644 at Topeka, Kansas in July, 2000. (Photo by Larry Tiffany, Collection of Lou Schmitz)

WP Insulated Box Car No. 66138 at Council Bluffs, Iowa, May 4, 1986 (Lou Schmitz)

WP box car No. 38659 at Topeka, Kansas, July 1999. (Larry Tiffany, Collection of Lou Schmitz)

WP Covered Hopper No. 11639, Topeka, Kansas, July 1, 1994. (Larry Tiffany, Collection of Lou Schmitz)

WP Covered Hopper No. 11687, Topeka, Kansas, May, 1997. (Larry Tiffany, Collection of Lou Schmitz)

WP Hopper Car No. 10946, Topeka, Kansas, October, 1998. (Larry Tiffany, Collection of Lou Schmitz)

Double Plug Door, outside braced box car 65495 with both Union Pacific lettering and insignia. Photographed at St. Paul, Minnesota in 1988. (Thomas A. Dorin)

Covered Airslide Hopper Car No. 11690 at Council Bluffs, June 3, 1984. (Lou Schmitz)

We can wrap up this section of the book with a WP caboose bringing up the rear of an all rail ore train ready to depart the C&NW Itasca yard in Superior, Wisconsin. (Thomas A. Dorin)

Bibliography

RAILWAY AGE Magazines from 1910 to 1985

MOODY'S RAILROAD OR TRANSPORTATION MANUALS, 1940 TO 1982

POOR'S RAILROAD VOLUMES, 1912 TO 1939

Western Pacific Mechanical Records and Equipment Diagrams

Western Pacific Railroad Passenger Time Tables:

> May 15, 1935
> July 20, 1939
> All, 1950
> April 27, 1952
> September 28, 1958
> January 1, 1969

Western Pacific Division Time Tables:

> Eastern Division, July 6, 1947 and April 24, 1960
> Western Division, July 6, 1947 and October 25, 1959
> Consolidated Western and Eastern Divisions, June 11, 1972
> Time Table No. 5, April 30, 1976
> System, October 25, 1981

AMTRAK Time Table, Summer, 1988

_____, "The Royal Gorge Passenger Train, MILEPOSTS, San Francisco,
California, Western Pacific Railroad Company, December, 1949.

Hutchinson, W. H., "A Streetcar Names Zephyrette," TRAINS, July, 1952

Kelly, John K., WESTERN PACIFIC, San Francisco, California: The Western Pacific
Railroad Company.

For more specific details, refer to Chapter Endnotes.

RECOMMENDATIONS FOR FUTHER READING AND RESEARCH

Crump, Spencer, WESTERN PACIFIC, THE RAILROAD THAT WAS BUILT TOO LATE, Los Angeles, California, Trans-Anglo Books, 1963.

Dunscomb, Guy L., and Fred A. Stindt, WESTERN PACIFIC STEAM LOCOMOTIVES, PASSENGER TRAINS AND CARS, Modesto, California: Privately Published, 1980.

Irions, Tom, "Still a Unique Shortline, PACIFIC NEWS, August, 1972.

Strapac, Joseph A. WESTERN PACIFIC DIESEL YEARS, Muncie, Indiana: Overland Models, Inc. 1980.

For a large number of articles refer to:

Wayner, Robert, ALL-TIME INDEX OF RAILROAD MAGAZINES, New York, New York: Wayner Publications, 1978

WP Color Section

(Above) No. 2262 pauses at Salt Lake City in anticipation of a new assignment. Note the color scheme for this particular unit, photographed on July 27, 1979. (Ryan Ballard, TLC Collection)

WP No. 3527 displays the darker color scheme of the GP40s at the very end of the 1970s, in fact, November 5, 1979 at Salt Lake City in this quick portrait of Western Pacific time. (Ryan Ballard, TLC Collection)

The orange decor on the nose of GP40, No. 3544, added much to the color scheme on the WP. It is January 16, 1980. (Ryan Ballard, TLC Collection)

Now here is a work of railroad art and magic in every sense of the word. Six F units are powering a freight near Pulga Canyon. It is September 29, 1959, and the power displays the two variations in color schemes that were observable on the A and the B units at that period of time. (TLC Collection)

A time frieght rolls out of a tunnel and on to an embankment with green waters in the foreground. It just goes to show that traveling by rail one can get the greatest views of the beautiful scenery. (March 16, 1970, R. J. Robl, TLC Collection)

(Below) GP40 No. 3519 shows off its colors as compared to the No. 3525 coupled to the rear. Note the orange nose as compared to the stripes on 3525. The motive power is between runs at Salt Lake City on July 13, 1980. (G. Pekkanen, TLC Collection)

110

What more could one ask for in terms of absolute beauty? A freight with 4 units for power, cruises along the incredible beauty of the Feather River and surrounding mountains and hills. It can be said that nothing can top the enjoyment of life than train watching in an incredible, fantastic beautiful scenic area. (Alan M. Miller, TLC Collection)

Speaking of viewing the magnificent beauty of Mother Earth, the California Zephyr was one of the best ways to travel and enjoy the scenery. The CZ is near Pulga, California on October 17, 1969. (Richard Wallin, TLC Collection)

Alco S4 No. 564 and S2 No. 560 rest for a moment between switching chores at Stockton. The two units are in the full orange color scheme on this October 7, 1976 Autumn Day. (TLC Collection)

F7 921D at Stockton on Jun3 26, 1973. (Steve Gartner, TLC Collection)

GP40-2 No. 3549 illustrates the paint scheme application on the left side of the unit with dark green and orange nose and lettering. No. 3549's portrait was taken at Topeka, Kansas on September 25, 1983, about two years in advance of the Union Pacific merger. (George N. Mence, TLC Collection)

GP40-2 No. 3553 MU'd with UP power at Salt Lake City in July, 1981. (G. Pekkanen,TLC Collection)

WP GP40 No. 3512 is on board with the Missouri Pacific as it is MU'd with MoPac power at Pueblo, Colorado on September 8, 1985. (TLC Collection)

It is 1970, and the California Zephyr is still the Real Rail Way to Travel. No. 17 is rolling through incredible scenery near Clio, California on March 16, 1970. (TLC Collection)

WP's 913 is in the Altamont siding on the Western Division on April 20, 1979. (TLC Collection)

Still another view of rail freight traveling through the mountain region of California with snow on the ground at the upper elevations. It is February, 1971. (TLC Collection)

GP40 No. 3514 in the dark green with orange nose, lettering and trim. (TLC Collection)

GP40 No. 3529 at Salt Lake City, September 4, 1983. (G. Pekkanen)

GP40 No. 3535 has a bit of decoration with snow on this cold January 28, 1984 day at Salt Lake City. (TLC Collection)

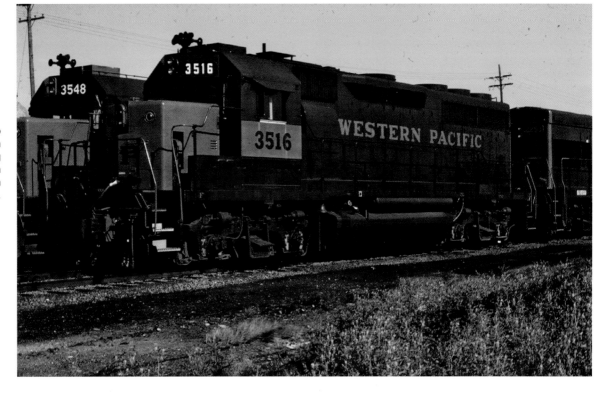

Motive power line up at Salt Lake City with GP40, No. 3516 taking front and center with GP40-2 No. 3548 in the background. (G. Pekkanen)

U30B No. 3059 is teamed up with GP7 No. 702 on the Garden Track at Stockton, California. (Roger W. Coleman, TLC Collection)

116

F7 No. 913 has accumulated a dusty face as it awaits its next freight run assignment at Salt Lake City on March 1, 1978. Sometimes working on the railroading could end up with quite a bit of dust, dirt, mud and anything else one can think of out on the road. (Jim Aldridge, TLC Collection)

A time freight is ready to spring into action with GP35, No. 3001 leading two other units at the Orville, California yard. Note the 700 series Geep to the right of the photo. (Steve Gartner, TLC Collection)

GP40 No. 3529 leads a freight on the Union Pacific main line at North Platte, Nebraksa on August 21, 1981. (TLC Collection)

Western Pacific No. 3535 leads a freight side by side with a Union Pacific freight at Salt Lake City on August 10, 1972. (W. D. Volkmer, TLC Collection)

GP40 No. 3526 between assignments at Oakland on October 21, 1976. (TLC Collection)

Western Pacific F7 No. 917 is at the Stockton Shops for some additional work, It is looking great. The Stockton shops were a crucial element for WP's motive power maintenance work. (Roger W. Coleman, TLC Collection)

The California Zephyr is rolling out of Tunnel No. 9 at Pulga, California on a very neat and sunny spring day in April, 1968. (R. J. Robl, TLC Collection)

SW9 No. 604 is between assignments at Stockton in this August, 1977 photo. (James Claflin, Electro Motive Division, TLC Collection)

GP40 No. 3524 at Oakland in May, 1971. (J. M. Seidl, TLC Collection)

Left side view of GP40, No. 3513 at Salt Lake City, November, 1981. (G. Pekkanen, TLC Collection)

U23B No. 2254 between runs at Salt Lake City, June, 1982. (G. Pakkanen, TLC Collection)

GP20 No. 2009 leads a time freight through the picturesque scenic area near Pulga, California. (TLC Collection)

The California Zephyr rolls along near Pulga, California in the Autumn Season of October, 1969. A great time for train travel with new levels of scenic viewing. (Richard R. Wallin, TLC Collection)

A view of the California Zephyr from the rear as it moves through the scenic area near Pulga in the Spring of 1968. (TLC Collection)

GP40 No. 3529 between assignments at Oakland, California in June, 1976. (TLC Collection)

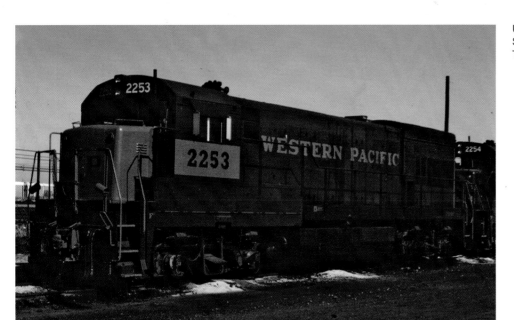

U23B No. 2253 between time freight runs at Salt Lake City in May, 1982. (G. Pekkanen, TLC Collection)

The U23Bs are brand new in the photo as they pause in Erie, Pennsylvania en route from the General Electric to the Western Pacific in June, 1972. (David S. Albrewczynski, TLC Collection)

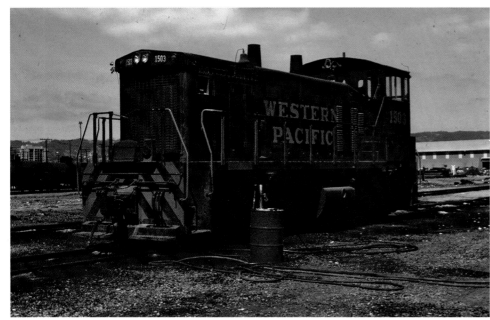

Left side view of SW1500 No. 1503 at Oakland in June, 1976. (TLC Collection)

F7 No. 920D powers a five car passenger extra consisting entirely of Southern Pacific passenger equipment including a combine in the Daylight Color Scheme. The train is pausing at Stockton on this Halloween Day in 1965. (Norton D. Clark, TLC Collection)

F7 919D along with a B unit lay over at Stockton for inspections in November, 1967. (TLC Collection)

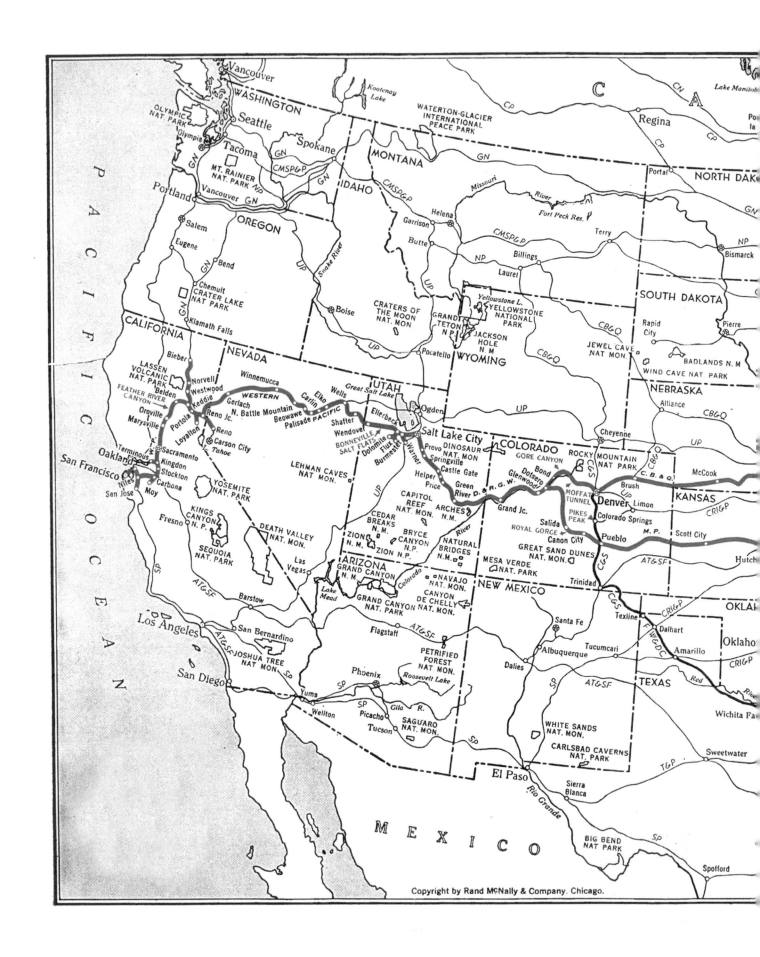